Kerrie Davies is a journalist and media academic at UNSW. She has written for *Collective* magazine, *Elle*, *Vogue Australia* and *The Weekend Australian Magazine*, among other media outlets. She is completing her Doctor of Arts (Literary Journalism) at the University of Sydney and is co-author of the *Colonial Australian Literary Journalism Database*.

A WIFE'S HEART

THE UNTOLD STORY OF BERTHA AND HENRY LAWSON

KERRIE DAVIES

UQP

First published 2017 by University of Queensland Press
PO Box 6042, St Lucia, Queensland 4067 Australia

www.uqp.com.au
uqp@uqp.uq.edu.au

Cover design by Christabella Designs
Cover images: Photograph of Bertha Lawson, 1898, photographer unknown. Published in
Journal of the Royal Australian Historical Society, vol. 55, no. 4, 1969. Letter from Bertha
Lawson to Henry Lawson, 25 July 1903, in Lothian Publishing Company records 1895–
1950, MS 6026, Box XX1A Lawson material, State Library Victoria. Used with permission
of State Library Victoria. Eucalyptus leaves © Aliaksei_7799/Shutterstock
Author photograph by Jake Starr
Typeset in 12/17 pt Adobe Garamond Pro by Post Pre-press Group, Brisbane
Printed in Australia by McPherson's Printing Group

This project has been assisted by the
Australian Government through
the Australia Council, its arts funding
and advisory body.

National Library of Australia
Cataloguing-in-Publication data is available at http://catalogue.nla.gov.au

ISBN
978 0 7022 5966 1 (pbk)
978 0 7022 5919 7 (ePDF)
978 0 7022 5920 3 (ePub)
978 0 7022 5921 0 (Kindle)

For my daughter, Ruby

I did not realise then the restlessness which always filled Harry's heart and soul, a state which was entirely due to the blood that ran in his veins — wanderer's blood.

Bertha Lawson, *My Henry Lawson* (1943)

IN THE SUPREME COURT
of New South Wales
Matrimonial Causes Jurisdiction.

In re HENRY LAWSON of Manly in the State
of New South Wales Author and Journalist
And BERTHA MARIE LOUISA LAWSON (formerly
BERTHA MARIE LOUISA BREDT. Spinster) his wife.[1]

On this third day of April in the year of our Lord
one thousand nine hundred and three, BERTHA MARIE
LOUISA LAWSON wife of HENRY LAWSON of Manly in the
State of New South Wales Author and Journalist being
duly sworn maketh oath and saith as follows.

1. I was on the fifteenth day of April A.D. One
thousand eigth [sic] hundred and ninety six, lawfully
married to HENRY LAWSON at Sydney in New South Wales
according to the rites of the Church of England.

2. I was born at Bairnsdale in the State of
Victoria and am at the present that is to say at
the date of the institution of this suit and have
for three years and upwards been domiciled in New
South Wales. My husband I was informed by him and
believe was born at Grenfell in the State of New
South Wales and is at the present time that is to
say at the date of the institution of this suit and
has been for three years and upwards been domiciled
in New South Wales.

3. I and my said husband have had issue of our said
marriage two children to wit JOSEPH HENRY LAWSON aged

five years and one month and BERTHA MARIE LOUISA
LAWSON aged three years and one month.

4. My husband has during three years and upwards been
an habitual drunkard and habitually been guilty of
cruelty towards me.

5. My husband has been guilty of cruelty towardsme
[*sic*].

6. The cruelty alleged in paragraphs four and five of
this. My affidavit consists of the acts and matters
following. That my husband during the last three
years struck me in the face and about the body and
blacked my eye and hit me with a bottle and attempted
to stab me and pulled me out of bed when I was ill
and purposely made a noise in my room when I was ill
and pulled my hair and repeatedly used abusive and
insulting language to me and was guilty of divers
other acts of cruelty to me whereby my health and
safety are endangered.

Bertha Marie Louise Lawson [handwritten signature]

Sworn by the Deponent on the day
and year first before written
Before me. At Sydney

[signature unclear]
A Commissioner for Affidavits
April 3rd, 1903[2]

Girlie,

Do try to forgive and forget. My heart is breaking and I can't live without you. Remember I was ill, very ill, and not responsible for what I said. It was all my fault. If I make you suffer, think how I have suffered. I have not touched a drink and am working hard. Don't think I'm a coward and afraid of the money. I have paid it into court and making plenty. Dearie I love you with all my heart and soul and will never say an unkind word to you again. Don't listen to friends and neighbours – listen to me.

I will bury the past if you can. Come to me tonight and save me. You don't know what I'm asking you to save me from. Let us have one more try for happiness. If I did not love you so much I might not have taken notice of little things. If you can't come, at least let little Bertha come to me 'till Monday. Don't let pride stand in your way.

Remember the happy days we had once. Only think of me as the man I was and will be again. Dearie I was kind – it was only that woman who wrecked our lives. Don't be influenced by two-faced mischief makers but come to your unhappy husband.

Forgive me and come to me and we'll be happy in spite of it all.

Harry (I'll write very hard until midnight).[3]

1

I slip into the salt water, my goggles clinging to my eyes. Sunbathing backpackers languish on daybeds along the pool's edge, the glass fence framing their burning bodies. Out on the harbour, divided from the pool by a timber boardwalk, Riviera speedboats cruise by, splashing Sydney's wealth.

Lingering at the end of the pool, I move aside as another swimmer strokes to a stop. He stands up and peers at the sky.

'This might ruin our day,' he says. Another storm is moving in. But it seems too early in the season for snap storms.

The storm keeps its distance but it shades Henry Lawson's statue, his most prominent memorial. Wet from the swim, and for once not in a hurry, I stop to scrutinise him.

Henry has weathered the summers well since he was unveiled in 1931. Sculpted in bronze by George Lambert, he stands atop a plinth of sandstone, with those big, sensitive eyes looking out over the Royal Botanic Garden and The Domain. The Henry Lawson Literary Society protested that the sculpture's location was too hidden away, arguing upon visiting the site that it was 'one of the very nooks the poet would have revelled in for contemplation and the writing of a set of verse, but certainly not the place for his monument; it is too unfrequented, too suggestive of obscurity'.[1]

At a preview of the plaster model, held at Lambert's studio, this Henry was described by critics as 'an imposing piece of sculpture in larger than life size', and a 'remarkable likeness'.[2] Lambert had first modelled Henry's head on that of Jim, the poet's son, who'd sat for the sculptor to help create the memorial to his father. The dog was modelled on a hound from a local rescue home. But then, prior to the showing in his Sydney studio, Lambert had replaced the first plaster head because it had fallen off overnight, onto the studio floor.[3] Henry was as fragile in the art made in his honour as he was in life.

Perhaps the Lawson society were right in saying that the statue is hidden away. Since I've read Bertha's affidavit, Henry looks more shadowy than ever.

Henry's hand seems to form around an invisible mug, perhaps of billy tea, or more likely a beer. At the unveiling, however, the Memorial Fund's chairperson said Lambert wanted to capture Henry's mannerism: 'Lawson's hand was not raised in gesticulation whilst reciting, but "so as to see a distant hill or as if to recall far horizons of memory" – a familiar gesture of the poet's.'[4]

Still looks like he wants a beer. The *Bulletin* cartoonist David Low apparently wanted Lawson's line, 'Beer makes you feel as you ought to feel without beer', as the statue's inscription.[5]

At the end of the path is Mrs Macquarie's Chair, where Henry Lawson and Bertha Bredt took their first stroll together late in 1895.

The ironies of Henry's statue multiply here in The Domain, where he stands today as Bertha wanted then – a figure of stability. If only Henry had been like his statue in life. But then Bertha wouldn't have been seduced by his poetry, by his literary beauty, by seeing herself as his muse, which her critics suggest she thought she was.

Once you become the wife, you are associated with domesticity rather than divine inspiration. Then come the divorce, the demands, the need. The lack.

On Christmas Day my daughter's father, Dan, posts on Facebook from LA airport. For 13-year-old Ruby, Facebook is also a father-positioning system. A jazz pianist, he is a five-star gypsy, working on luxury cruise ships that take him a hemisphere away. When Ruby was little, she tried to follow him on a world map on her wall until it was a mass of scribbles curling at the corners.

We've spent the days leading up to Christmas with Ruby's aunt, Mariana, who recently split from her husband. Our friendship has endured my divorce from her twin brother five years ago, even though such convulsions usually result in divorce from the ex's family as well. She has a white cottage near the beach, into which she's squeezed her four children after moving out from a waterfront mansion. By Boxing Day, they and Ruby are in a sunburnt slump around the Xbox in the living room. Outside, plastic strings of Christmas lights hang in the sun. Despite the post-Christmas mess, the cottage has a feminine feel, and a resoluteness. Artworks that Mariana's husband disliked are now hung around the house.

She stacks the dishwasher with listless intent. 'I'm tired,' she says. 'I live on a shoestring. The credit card's gone. It's hard doing everything – looking after the kids, the house – and working as well.'

He's paying child support and at least she had some savings when they separated. She is managing to pay the rent, so she knows it could be worse. But it's still such a shock.

When I go back to town Ruby stays on with her cousins at the beach for the following week. Even though she is a teenager now, when she is away the quietness is unsettling. Sometimes I still panic – have I forgotten to pick her up? She is an ever present responsibility in my thoughts, if not in my presence. When she was little, a boyfriend once told me unthinkingly: 'She is a burden on you.'

'She is my child,' I snapped.

Imagine Bertha, as a new single mother, having a similar response. She is in my thoughts now too. On the day the affidavit was lodged in the Divorce Court, Friday 3 April 1903, *The Sydney Morning Herald* reported on a drought relief concert, and that the Women's Social and Political League had met, and that a suspected attempted wife murderer who had cut his own throat had survived.[6]

History is what you are told, what you remember and what you learn. Once I'd been told, in an offhand conversation with a literary friend, that Henry did not (or could not, as his supporters defend) pay regular child support – from that day on, Henry was no longer a long-ago poet to me. He was a father to children. He was a husband. There was a wife, who was clearly bringing up the children with little help.

I keep wondering, how did Bertha live as a separated, single mother in the early 20th century, when women had barely won the vote? Did the Divorce Court support her? Or Henry?

Henry was cruel, Bertha alleged.
An habitual drunkard. Blacked my eye. Endangered me.
The questions keep doing laps in my head.

2

Included in a letter from Henry Lawson to Bertha Bredt at her home at McNamara's Bookshop, 5 March 1896:

After All

The brooding ghosts of Australian night have gone from
    the bush and town;
My spirit revives in the morning breeze, though it died
    when the sun went down;
The river is high and the stream is strong, and the grass is
    green and tall,
And I fain would think that this world of ours is a good
    world after all.

The light of passion in dreamy eyes, and a page of truth
    well read,
The glorious thrill in a heart grown cold of the spirit
    I thought was dead,

A song that goes to a comrade's heart, and a tear of pride
  let fall –
And my soul is strong! and the world to me is a grand
  world after all!

Let our enemies go by their old dull tracks, and theirs be
  the fault or shame
(The man is bitter against the world who has only himself
  to blame);
Let the darkest side of the past be dark, and only the good
  recall;
For I must believe that the world, my dear, is a kind world
  after all.

It well may be that I saw too plain, and it may be I was blind;
But I'll keep my face to the dawning light, though the devil
  may stand behind!
Though the devil may stand behind my back, I'll not see
  his shadow fall,
But read the signs in the morning stars of a good world
  after all.

Rest, for your eyes are weary, girl – you have driven the
  worst away –
The ghost of the man that I might have been is gone from
  my heart to-day;
We'll live for life and the best it brings till our twilight
  shadows fall;
My heart grows brave, and the world, my girl, is a good
  world after all.[1]

⋏

My copy of Bertha's memoir, *My Henry Lawson*,[2] has a watermarked cover and the spine is flaking; yet somehow, like a bad marriage, it stays together. The fragile pages give her account of Henry's early life with his mother, the feminist Louisa Lawson, and his father, Peter, on a parched property in New South Wales. Peter panned for glints of gold and Louisa tried to turn the land into a farm, only to feel more fenced in by the restrictions of rural life. Foreseeing a future of drought-blighted drudgery, Louisa instead took their youngest son, Peter, and daughter, Gertrude, to Sydney. The elder Henry soon followed.

In late 1895 he met Bertha near her stepfather's bohemian bookshop, McNamara's, which smelt of beer and onions.[3] She said she wavered and resisted Henry at first. He'd been about to go to New Zealand; feeling deflated by her refusal, he decided to go off as he'd planned. But then, according to Bertha, no sooner had he docked in New Zealand than he caught a ship back.

She wrote, 'He pleaded with me to be married right away. I refused. Next morning, I received his poem, "After All" and a letter ...'[4]

However, there was still Mrs McNamara to convince. Bertha's younger sister, Hilda, 17, was already dating Jack Lang and now here was Henry, 28, eyeing Bertha, only 19. Mothers are suspicious of gypsies, writers and artists; Mrs McNamara may have been the 'Mother of the Labor Movement',[5] and a bohemian herself, but the politics of marriage suitability were quite different.

In 'Memories', Bertha's contribution to the anthology *Henry Lawson by His Mates*, she recalled:

After we had known each other for about six weeks we became engaged. But my dear little mother did not approve of the match nor did other members of my family. Harry was very deaf and delicate. He had no worldly goods – nothing but his literary genius – and there were obstacles. But we did not heed these, being sure that together we could overcome everything.[6]

She was more candid with a friend, author Ruth Park, who with husband D'Arcy Niland co-wrote a radio play in 1952, *The Courtship of Henry Lawson*. In an interview with an elderly Bertha, Ruth recorded on gold paper in fast, pencilled notes that Bertha's mother 'blew up Henry', saying 'she was too young' and 'You've got no home, nothing settled. How can you provide for her?' Mrs McNamara had even locked the door, but Bertha scrambled down the window. Bertha said that Henry was resolute: 'I'm going to marry her and that's all there is to it' and he 'would give up the drink' if Mrs McNamara gave her consent.[7]

When I told my father a century later that I was marrying a musician, he said, 'Does he have an earring? Who will look after you?' Looking back at the photos of our wedding, I see a slightly stunned girl in a white dress, and a husband who, like the photos, has faded away.

Henry is part of the city. He is a sudden appearance during a stroll. Walking from the city through the gardens, you can exit through the Henry Lawson Gate to get to Mrs Macquarie's Chair and the harbourside pool. A postcard featuring a drawing of Henry Lawson's headstone on the cliff top at Waverley Cemetery is on a stand at Bondi. On a bushwalk around Berry's Bay a verse from his poem 'Kerosene Bay' is inscribed in the concrete. A lady says loudly on her mobile phone, 'I didn't know you were up here! I'm going to tell my sister, who lives right down in Henry Lawson Drive.'

He keeps turning up. In Canberra a gold cast of his long, emaciated writing hand, as sculpted by his friend Nelson Illingworth, is in a glass-encased display at the National Library of Australia. There's an annual Henry Lawson Festival in Grenfell, where he was born. Before Gallipoli, he was the poet who created mateship. The Dickens of the bush. He's been mythologised, anthologised and analysed.

Bertha has been forgotten. Filed away in boxes of letters, birthday cards and notes.

Ghost signs remain on the streets. A leather-goods shop sign is bleached into brick on a Castlereagh Street wall. Further along, at number 221, is the site of McNamara's bohemian bookshop, the default living room for writers, politicians and intellectuals, including one lanky poet, Henry Lawson, and a future state premier, Jack Lang. Where once communist posters hung in the demolished bookshop, the Bank of Sydney now displays its interest rates in its windows, which are painted a plain steel-grey. Scaffolding covers the nearby corner where Bertha said she first met Henry, as he loped down the street on his way to the bookshop. She told Ruth Park that she was impressed by his 'big marvellous eyes' that were a 'deep brown'. She called them 'the most wonderful eyes I've seen', and spoke of Henry's 'soft voice' and 'quiet smile'.[8]

Writing about Bertha in her memoir *Fishing in the Styx*, Park asked Henry's friend, New Zealand journalist Tom Mills: 'Why did Henry fall for Bertha?'

'Oh,' he said decisively, 'it was the shape that caught Henry.'

D'Arcy, when he heard, laughed. 'Sounds like a music-hall song!' But it was true that even at seventy-five or -six small round Bertha had an hour-glass shape, probably with the aid of corsets.[9]

Henry, a corseted Bertha and her escort, the bookshop's assistant Karl Lindgrist, made their way to Mrs Macquarie's Chair, where Lindgrist left them alone. He must have felt miffed at Henry weaving between the shapely Bertha and him; Bertha told Park that Karl was also keen on her shape.

More than a century later, I walk through the Botanic Garden to the Chair, and wonder if the bats shat on Henry and Bertha too. There has been a campaign to move the bats on as they are destroying the old trees, but they cling to the branches above.

Along the Circular Quay boardwalk a plaque is dedicated to Henry's confidant, Dame Mary Gilmore. She said she knew the truth about Henry and Bertha, providing an alternative narrative of the romance. Whom to believe?

The Dame argued:

> Last week (1922) Frank McGrath of the old Edinburgh Hotel – in those days the writers' rendez-vous – said, speaking voluntarily: 'And by Jove! don't I remember his marriage! She chased him till she got him! She never let him alone till she caught him … She threatened to commit suicide or something, and said her father was going to turn her out into the streets if he wouldn't marry her!' It was what Henry himself told me

once in a broken-hearted moment when his wife had been particularly cruel to him.[10]

Ruth Park and D'Arcy Niland were friends with both Mary and Bertha in their later lives. Comparing the two women in her memoir, Park observed: 'We both found Bertha very likeable. She was durable, humorous and kindly. My impression was that, when young, she had probably been a voluptuous little bundle. Still she gave off that indefinable fragrance that attracts men.'[11]

Henry's publisher, George Robertson, upon learning of the engagement, told his personal assistant, Rebecca Wiley:

> She had great big hazel eyes, and shining with excitement; they were undoubtedly very much in love with each other ... but ... I knew Henry even then was a confirmed drinker; had at times a very nasty temper, and all the other things that go to make a genius very difficult to live with.

He foresaw 'nothing but tragedy in it for both of them'.

Robertson was so concerned, he pulled Bertha aside:

> I spent a whole morning pleading with her not to take this irrevocable step. I told her I had three little girls of my own, and I'd rather see them dead, than to marry a temperamental genius, who was a drunkard as well. It was all in vain, she knew she could keep him straight, love would do it, and so on.[12]

Henry's mother, Louisa, sided with the worried publisher and with Bertha's mother. 'The woman who cannot give a better reason for marrying than that she is in love, is likely to come to grief. It is not *that* she loves, but *why* or *what* she loves, that is the all important question,' she warned prophetically in 'Unhappy Love Matches', published in her feminist paper, *The Dawn*, in 1889.[13]

Who really knows? Perhaps their daughter, who was christened Bertha Louisa after her mother and grandmother, but nicknamed Barta by Henry. Her unpublished notes about her parents nestle among other Lawson family folders in the Mitchell Library:

> It is certain she [Mother] and Dad did love each other ... They were young and full of hope. They were eager for the future ... But it was he who saw the situation that might lie before them both – not Mother, headstrong, eager, impetuous, wanting nothing to stand in her way. Dad saw it. J Le Gay [Brereton] told me that he came to him for help. He was so worried. He loved her. He wanted to marry her. He was afraid. If he couldn't depend on himself, what would happen? Calamity for him but most of all for her. He had more than half made up his mind to get out of Sydney and go back to the bush. He did not know what to do. J Le Gay told me, he said: 'Look Henry, I've known you to do silly things, but I've never known you to run away before.' Dad thanked him and went off ... Dad saw very clearly, even when he could not help himself, in the tragic hopelessness of his own situation, to do anything about it.[14]

The hopelessness.

Bertha recalled that on 15 April 1896 Henry arrived to where she was living with Mrs Schaebel in the inner-city suburb of Newtown:

My trousseau was all ready, and we were to be married at St Stephen's, Newtown. But Harry had not been able to win over the family though he did obtain my mother's written consent. On 15 April he arrived early in the morning and begged me to come to town and meet a dear friend of his. He said 'I want you to look very nice, so put on your wedding dress to please me.' But I was horrified at the thought of wearing my wedding dress before my wedding. However, we finally agreed on my travelling dress – a green silk frock with a brown hat wreathed in poppies!

We told Mrs Schaebel we'd be back by half-past three. When we got to town Harry showed me another indignant letter that he had received. He was very troubled and said that he felt convinced that unless we married straightaway, we would be separated in the end. So he had arranged with a clergyman to marry us privately that day, if only I was willing. He showed me his special licence. But I told him that it was impossible. Our wedding had been arranged, the guests invited and all plans fixed for our Blue Mountain honeymoon. In any case I thought Mrs Schaebel should be told. But Harry said we could be married and then go straight out and tell her. He was so afraid, in view of all the opposition, that something would come between us; he had a strong intuition that we might be parted. And loving him so dearly I felt that there was much truth in what he said and I consented. We went straight round to the clergyman's home and were married – a member of his family acting as a witness.

We started off afterwards for the Newtown tram, but Harry said no, we must go out in state in a cab as befitted the occasion. So we drove out to Newtown to find Mrs Schaebel very angry, because I was late Harry bent down and kissed her and said, 'That doesn't matter, because she's my wife now. Here is our certificate.' Mrs Schaebel was most upset, and asked what she was to do about the bridesmaids and the guests. He said, 'Never mind, just say we are married.' She was very indignant, but because she was very fond of us both she forgave us in the end.[15]

Henry, 28, wrote his occupation as 'journalist' on the wedding certificate and Bertha, 19, was a 'gentlewoman'. Her parents and his mother knew nothing of the ceremony. Neither, it seems, did their families or Henry's publishers, although Bertha says that Henry obtained her mother's consent: 'He had wheedled the signature out of my mother. Perhaps she felt as I did, that to have refused him when we loved one another so much, would have broken his heart.'[16]

The marriage cost one pound, which Henry borrowed from his friend Louis Becke, a novelist and short-story writer who wrote about travels in the South Pacific.

Mrs Isabel Byers, who looked after Henry in later years, believed that Henry loved Bertha, but he rushed into the marriage. She said Henry told her:

> that he was not deeply in love with Miss Bredt at the time he married her but that as time went on, he grew to love her more and more …
>
> Miss Bredt was unhappy at home when she came to know Lawson, and that Lawson out of sympathy for her took her away from her home and placed her under the care of Mrs Schaebel. Mrs Lawson's brother said this was really a case of abduction as Miss Bredt was not of age and that Lawson on hearing of this arranged for a hasty marriage.[17]

If Bertha was disappointed and dismayed with the rushed plainness of the day, or that she did not wear her dress, she did not reveal it in her memoir. When you think about it, she rarely reveals anything at all.

Bertha did tell Ruth Park that, upon being shown the marriage certificate, her mother shrieked, 'You pair of lunatics. Henry Lawson get out of my house!'[18]

Bertha also recalled: 'We spent a happy day together and in the evening went to a hotel near St Andrews Cathedral – I think it was the Town Hall Hotel ... On the following morning we went hunting for rooms in Darlinghurst ... in Forbes St, we found a tiny flat ...'[19]

The Royal Town Hall Hotel, where Henry and Bertha spent their wedding night, was periodically fined for Sunday trading, but is now a 7-Eleven store. At the nearby Edinburgh and Castle pub that Mary Gilmore dubbed 'Botany Bay bohemia's favourite meeting place', mottled tiles decorate the outside walls and a chalkboard advertises happy hour. A conservative crowd of tradies, tourists and punters hang around the bar and the betting screen. Bohemia has moved on.

A monograph of Harold Cazneaux's photographs of Sydney in the early 20th century captures washing hanging between dusty lines, a wet North Sydney street dominated by a town-hall spire, and a row of hansom cabs with docile horses waiting for rides in a city with over 3000 pubs and 288,000 people.[20] Artist and cartoonist Norman Lindsay drew wharfies, policemen, Chinese and hatted men at the Quay, where he went to the *Bulletin* offices nearby and ate at cheap cafes.[21] As today there was constant public debate about drunkenness brought on by 'the Australian habit of shouting'. And there was talk, always, of the weather: in summer, snap thunderstorms, a restless heat and downpours that streamed down the streets.

The day after the wedding, they went to the *Bulletin* offices. Imagine Henry holding Bertha's hand on the way to the office, the horns of the harbour ferries sounding like a warning. *The Bulletin*'s editor, JF Archibald, like George Robertson, was well aware that Henry was high maintenance, although he was still writing and being published regularly. An achieving alcoholic.

Earlier in the decade, Archibald had sent Henry out into the Australian bush to write about the drought-damaged landscape, but also because he was already concerned about Henry's health. Archibald asked Henry's friend and fellow writer EJ Brady: 'What's the matter with Lawson? … he is coming here in the morning with tobacco-juice running down his jaw, smelling of stale beer, and he has begun to write about "The Rocks".'[22]

A picture of the two men together is as candid as a photograph from 1918 can be. Henry, tall and lanky in a suit, leans into an older, smaller and still impeccably dressed Archibald. Henry looks like he is listening hard, perhaps because of his partial deafness, which developed in childhood, and also perhaps because Archibald was his mentor.[23]

At the *Bulletin* office with his bride, Henry announced that they had married.

Bertha recounted that Archibald stepped forward. 'We wish you well,' he said.

'Is this really true?' literary critic AG Stephens asked. 'And not a joke of Harry's?'

'It is quite true,' Bertha assured him. 'We were married yesterday. I'm going to try and make him happy.'

Stephens squeezed her hand. 'I hope he is going to try and make you happy.'

Bertha wrote:

> This announcement was like a bolt from the blue; it staggered everyone, to Harry's joy; but it upset me a little to have us regarded as freaks. But I found it was not I who astonished them, but the fact I had married a poet genius whom they regarded, apparently, as a man who could never make an income to maintain a home.[24]

Soon after the wedding, the Lawsons left Sydney for a short-lived stint in the outskirts of the gold-rush town of Perth. It was a sprawling makeshift settlement, and they lived in a flimsy, patchwork hessian tent on a floor of upturned corrugated-iron cases. The water was contaminated, and they had an oil drum for an oven.

Bertha recalled that Henry was keen to dig for gold but a friend, Smiler Hales, advised him that 'it would be madness to bring a young woman out there'.[25] The couple stayed in Perth. While they were in the west, Henry's book *While the Billy Boils* was published but the royalties didn't assist their finances. Gold was only a glimmer, a rush of hope, and their hunt for wealth turned back to the intangible gold in Henry's mind. They sold their camp for 35 pounds and returned to Sydney.

Henry's *Bulletin* colleague Bertram Stevens became friendly with them after their return:

> She [Mrs Lawson] was young & attractive, her eyes being particularly fine, her voice soft & rich. She was dressed neatly

(she told me afterwards it was her wedding dress she had on that night). As we walked home afterwards she talked to me as one who was devoted to Henry but had already discovered the inconvenience of having a genius for a husband …

He [Henry] had some social ambitions & would like to have had a comfortable home for his wife, but he was too careless & too selfish to make any sacrifice to provide one. He had generous impulses but no steadfastness of purpose in any direction.

At this time Lawson certainly had a good deal of respect for his wife, recognised that she was trying to keep him from drink for his own good. He amused himself by dodging her efforts. He did not disclose to her all he earned & on *Bulletin* paydays he would hide money in his hat & boots & plant a few sixpences in corners of the room. When those tricks failed, he used to have small deposits of cash with a friendly barmaid to provide against dry days.[26]

Stevens said he tried mostly to keep Henry, and himself, relatively sober but fell foul of Bertha when they arrived home raucous and late: they were met by an 'avenging' Mrs Lawson at the gate. 'Henry blurted out something else whereupon I laughed – she didn't. Women haven't any sense of humour … As Henry persisted in departing from the sober path, his wife wanted to get him away from Sydney.'[27]

Bertha presented herself as the steerer of their marriage in these early years, searching for opportunities for financial stability but also wanting to 'leave him free to write'.[28] She turned to Archibald for help, as he had been Henry's patron for his Bourke expedition chronicling the drought in 1892. Imagine Archibald, dressed in a suit that reflected his Francophile impulses, regarding Bertha in his *Bulletin* office. Archibald perhaps recalled why he had first sent Henry bush, where bars were in different towns rather than in different streets, and where Henry could be inspired rather than intoxicated.

Yet there may have been another reason for Bertha's determination to move away. A 'shape' had caught Henry's eye at sculptor Nelson Illingworth's studio. Depending on which version you read, Hannah Thornburn may have been a 'rather plain, delicate' girl.[29] Or she may have been barely five foot, with red hair and grey eyes, a full mouth that artists liked to paint, and slender, 'like a clinging vine'.[30] Hannah was a bookseller's daughter, a Sunday school teacher, and an artist's model for Henry's friend, the curly-haired, poncho-wearing Illingworth. Nicknamed Buster, he'd also sculpted Norman Lindsay's second wife, Rose Soady. Rose described how, when modelling at the Illingworth household, she passed through the kitchen where Buster's wife was fanning herself and ignoring the woman going to her husband while the children argued over who would do the washing-up. Henry must have walked through that kitchen, and come upon Hannah sensuously wrapped in a cloak in between poses. Henry's biographers – their hardbacks now with dust hanging off them – range from those convinced that Henry was in love with a real rival to Bertha to those wondering if the new relationship was only a creation of his fertile, romantic mind.

3

From a letter dated 25 June 1897, to Hugh Maccallum, Angus &
Robertson, written from Mangamaunu, Kaikoura:

I felt like writing to you, somehow, perhaps because of your
kind reference to Mrs Lawson. I knew she was a gem, from the
first. I was right in that, as in most other things where drink
did not madden my instinct. She is a favourite everywhere and
worshipped here ...

I want to show some of my kind relatives (who never assisted
me or thought of me except perhaps as a soft idiotic fool to get
money and work out of) who advised Bertha against me from
the first, and kindly told her all my worst points – whilst, on the
other hand, and in common with one or two good but mistaken
friends, they persuaded me against being 'trapped' and ruining
my prospects when 'I might marry money and –'

I want to show them, if they be worth showing, that I have
made a success of my married life – and hers. I think I've married

money, too, as well as fame, but that will be seen. And I want to show the true friends, bushmen and others, who trusted and believed in me through it all – I want for their sake to write myself up to the top of the Australian gum …

With kindest regards from Mrs Lawson and myself.

Yours truly,
Henry Lawson[1]

With or without Hannah Thornburn as an impetus, Henry and Bertha arrived in Wellington, New Zealand, in April 1897, with Henry's books their only assets. In the ragged pages of her memoir, Bertha wrote that, as in Perth, she and Henry were again 'stranded in a strange town':

> I realised that my dreams when I sailed with Harry for Western Australia as a bride had been far from realised. We had made two voyages and gained nothing by the changes. I did not realise then the restlessness which always filled Harry's heart and soul, a state which was entirely due to the blood that ran in his veins – wanderer's blood.[2]

Henry had brought a letter of recommendation from Archibald, and previous acquaintance with the New Zealand politician Edward Tregear. He 'became our dear friend', Bertha wrote.[3] They initially stayed with Tom Mills, the New Zealand journalist who told Ruth Park that 'they were fighting like wildcats' during their stay.[4]

Bertha said she went on her own to the New Zealand government offices, where she was introduced to the Minister for Education, whose staff offered Bertha and Henry a Maori school position, with Henry as teacher and Bertha as his assistant, even though neither had taught anything in their lives. But another of Henry's biographers, WH Pearson – there are so many of them – researched in New Zealand and thinks that Henry was the one who met the Education Minister, as he is sceptical any minister would make such an appointment without meeting the poet.[5]

Regardless, Bertha, writing three decades later in *Henry Lawson by His Mates*, remembered their time in New Zealand as being among the happiest periods in their marriage. 'I came away with our first month's salary,' she said of the interview, and they used the money to set up their new life. Her duties as assistant were to instruct the women and children 'in hygiene, and to teach them how to sew', an art she says she had never conquered herself. Bertha bustled home to tell Henry, who, upon hearing he was to be a teacher, 'laughed very heartily, and took it as a great joke. He said, "Well, when do we start, and where?"'[6]

The truth keeps shifting like a sandbank.

A webcam surf forecast for Mangamaunu shows a swell breaking on black rocks, just as Bertha would have seen in 1897. She recalled:

> We arrived in the beautiful little town of Kaikoura, and drove to the schoolhouse. Mangamaunu was about eleven miles away, and when we arrived my hopes went down to zero. I had expected some sort of settlement, but found it was just a Maori pah beside the sea. It was most picturesque with the snow-covered Kaikouras behind us and the lonely ocean breaking on the rugged, rocky coast ... Between the mountains and the sea

was a flax morass with the schoolhouse situated on a slight rise. A few Maori whares were scattered in this flax swamp, but the main pah was on a high hill above the school ...

When we arrived at the schoolhouse, the Maoris came forward to greet us, one carrying some kumera (sweet potatoes) and another bearing a plate of wild pig. There were about fifty of them – all ages, from infants in arms to old tattooed warriors of eighty. The girls were beautiful and appealed to me with their wonderful dark eyes. I was enraptured with the Maori babies.

The Lawsons took over the existing schoolhouse and cottage, which had a neglected garden in the paddock next to it. In between teaching the children, with Henry sticking his head in occasionally to check how it was going, she made a home:

I took the outer covering off our new mattress and made red and white striped blinds of that. Harry cut bracken and placed our mattress on a high pile of the fern. And there we just camped for a while – cooking in our billy-can and frying-pan ... Harry got timber from Kaikoura and made a corner wardrobe and the other things we needed. He also made two very nice chairs from the cement casks. I covered them with cretonne, and they looked quite pretty. I bought flax mats from the Maoris. Together we stained and painted chairs, tables and floors, and with the white flax mats and an abundance of beautiful New Zealand clematis and wild flowers, we had quite a charming home.[7]

In one of their earliest conversations, when they were planning their future, Bertha said Henry *never* wanted a house decorated with cretonne – a heavy, printed cotton that covered furniture.[8] It must have represented domesticity to him, a static way of life.

Perhaps it was the isolation, the cretonne-covered furniture, their corroding companionship, or being just too far from a pub, but after a year in Mangamaunu the Lawsons resigned from their isolated teaching post, with Henry blaming 'the loneliness ... affecting Mrs Lawson's health'.[9] Bertha insisted that 'the loneliness didn't bother me'. In fact, she claimed: 'Harry was thoroughly contented and a great deal of his best work was done here ... We were ideally happy, like two children in a Garden of Eden.'[10] She added, as if defending her decision, and the location as a writer's retreat, that it was in New Zealand that Henry wrote another defining classic of his career, *Joe Wilson and his Mates*.

But Edens are fleeting paradises. The deciding factor for Bertha seems to have been the impending birth of their first baby. When she was seven months pregnant, they sold their possessions, or gave them away, as wanderers do. They returned to Wellington, where, just before Bertha was due to give birth, an earthquake rocked the city. Bertha remembered it as 'a terrifying experience ... We were offered another Maori school near Auckland, but Harry decided against it, as I was not yet strong, and we made up our minds to come home.'[11]

A baby also implies domesticity, a static way of life.

When Ruby was born, soon after we'd been living in London, Dan initially embraced the staticness. When she was nine months old, he cared for Ruby while I returned to work as a journalist then news editor. Ruby crawled around the piano while he practised. He brought her into the office en route to gigs, where she played with the foreign editor's red shoes under her desk as I finished up. My editor at the time was intrigued, and asked me to write a story about house husbands. Dan posed with Ruby in his arms, with other at-home fathers I found. It was static, domestic. A cretonne-covered life.

Biographer Denton Prout writes that Henry described his and Bertha's growing tension in the famous short story 'Water Them Geraniums'.[12] Published in *Joe Wilson and His Mates*, the short story was inspired by their nights in the schoolhouse. Henry thinly disguised Bertha as 'Mary', and observed that his wife had changed. But Henry did not recognise his own role in her rapid maturity, as well as her pregnancy:

> Mary didn't seem able to eat. She sat on the three-legged stool by the fire, though it was warm weather, and kept her face turned from me. Mary was still pretty, but not the little dumpling she had been: she was thinner now. She had big dark hazel eyes that shone a little too much when she was pleased or excited. I thought at times that there was something very German about her expression; also something aristocratic about the turn of her nose, which nipped in at the nostrils when she spoke. There was nothing aristocratic about me. Mary was German in figure and walk. I used sometimes to call her 'Little Duchy' and 'Pigeon Toes'. She had a will of her own, as shown sometimes by the obstinate knit in her forehead between the eyes.
>
> Mary sat still by the fire, and presently I saw her chin tremble.
> 'What is it, Mary?'
> She turned her face farther from me. I felt tired, disappointed, and irritated – suffering from a reaction.

'Now, what is it, Mary?' I asked; 'I'm sick of this sort of thing. Haven't you got everything you wanted? You've had your own way. What's the matter with you now?'

'You know very well, Joe.'

'But I *don't* know,' I said. I knew too well.

She said nothing.

'Look here, Mary,' I said, putting my hand on her shoulder, 'don't go on like that; tell me what's the matter.'

'It's only this,' she said suddenly, 'I can't stand this life here; it will kill me!'

I had a pannikin of tea in my hand, and I banged it down on the table.

'This is more than a man can stand!' I shouted. 'You know very well that it was you that dragged me out here ...'[13]

Their marriage had already changed the relationship from romance to resentment.

Isn't it how it always goes, however hard you try? Or is it because you try too hard?

I think about Bertha in New Zealand, and how their daughter wrote her own memories of her parents. Barta said her mother 'faced life always with confidence and courage' and showed 'kindness' and 'extraordinary charm'. She was 'enchanting', 'inspired love' and had 'magnetic and compelling fascination'. She was generous with an impulsive readiness in friendship.

But her daughter also wrote, as only a daughter can, of her mother's dominating strength, volatility, her high emotion, her swift temper, her need to guide, her passionate possessiveness, her demand for leadership. This made life fragile and exhausting for them all at times.

I'm rattled. Am I angelicising Bertha? Have I fallen for the martyred single mother, having been a single mother myself for most of my daughter's life? Reflecting my thoughts, Barta went on, 'These things were quite unknown to the many who came to her. They made the rich and complicated pattern of her life. Few people saw the underlying turmoil in her. It was my part to watch for the danger signals.'[14]

I'm on watch.

4

On the corner of another Sydney street is an old two-storey building painted grey with a discreet sign, 'Tierney House'. A smoker leans on the rail of the wheelchair ramp at the Ice Street entrance. As it turns out, this is a care centre for the homeless, offering health and outreach services. There were terraces down both streets once, but the homes across the road from the smoking man were resumed, and now there's a gap, where tankers park to fill the towering oxygen cylinders that supply the hospital opposite.

The avenue's remaining row of outpatient clinics and hospital buildings soften to workers' cottages, side-by-side survivors of the street's metamorphosis into one of Sydney's largest hospitals. It was on the corner of Ice and Great Barcom streets that in 1898 Henry's writer mates formed the Dawn and Dusk Club – named after Victor Daley's 1898 volume of poetry, *At Dawn and Dusk*.

Henry and Bertha had returned to Sydney with their baby, Joseph, nicknamed Jim, soon after his birth. Bertram Stevens said:

the arrival of the baby sobered Henry but the inevitable restlessness seized him that he had to get back to Sydney again. A day or two after return I met him & his wife in King St. He had grown a reddish-brown beard & was carrying the baby. For some time afterwards, he seemed steady & sober.[1]

But the soberness strayed away again after Lawson and his friends founded the Dawn and Dusk Club. Henry thought of the club's motto, 'Roost high and crow low'.[2] *Bulletin* writer Jim Philp, who edited Sydney's Chinese newspaper, wrote the club rules in Chinese. It sounds a lot of fun.

Oh, it was, said George Taylor, who wrote about the club in his 1918 memoir, *Those Were the Days*. He outlined the purity of a true bohemian club:

> Bohemian Clubs are invariably started by poets, artists, and other such impecunious personages; and in order that soul may commune with soul alone, the Philistine is always debarred.
>
> The poetic ones are so unpractical as to forget that it is the 'soulless Philistine' who keeps poetry and art alive by his purse. The absence of the detestable Philistine also deprives Bohemian clubs of the needful £ s. d., which explains why a Bohemian institution generally had a brief but merry life …
>
> The idea [of the Dawn and Dusk Club] was hatched in the home of Fred Broomfield, 'the Ever-Merry,' who was then sub-editor of 'The Bulletin.'
>
> It was a club composed of living or 'material' and departed or 'spiritual' Duskers. The former were such jovial souls as Victor Daley, elected 'Symposiarch'; Fred J. Broomfield, the 'Arch-Dusker'; 'Heptarchs' Henry Lawson, whose first book of

verse had just appeared; Jim Philp, a mine of humor, afterwards Commercial Editor of the 'Brisbane Courier'; C. Lindsay, Journalist; Nelson Illingworth, Sculptor; Bertram Stevens, who was later Editor of 'The Lone Hand'; Frank Mahoney, Artist; and the writer [George Taylor].[3]

Tom Roberts, future NSW premier William Holman and writer Randolph Bedford, according to George, all 'drifted in occasionally to feast at the banquet of wit and jingles' at the Dawn and Dusk Club.[4]

A spiritual Dusker was elected by ballot at the beginning of every meeting and given a vacant chair for their guest spot. Among those elected on different nights were Shakespeare, Montaigne, Rabelais, Thackeray, Balzac and Aristophanes. George recalled: 'Some others were nominated, amongst whom were Virgil, Dante, Milton, and Dr. Johnson, but, though great men, they had not much humor to boast of, hence they were not eligible for membership ...' Ditto for Walt Whitman, Verlaine, Socrates and Beethoven. Byron came close: he 'was considered to have every qualification for membership, but after a heated debate he was blackballed because of his selfishness'.[5]

Favourite meeting places, when someone could pay the bill, were Giovanni's wine cellar and the Hole in the Wall bar near Central station. Other times it was a pub counter lunch and beer, or plentiful prawns and BYO on the beach.[6]

George said the only other club worth joining was the 'Sacred Six' artists' club. Its members sketched models and everyone was desperate to get into it, but you weren't accepted without formal art training. Henry had done some coach painting in his youth, and briefly returned to the trade in Perth, but this was not enough. George, though, a cartoonist and journalist, was proud to be one of the six who sketched the women he called 'Bohemian girls', after he had convinced the other artists of his talent by sketching plaster heads.

Hannah Thornburn and Rose Soady, posing for Buster Illingworth and Norman Lindsay, were Bohemian girls, as was George's favourite model at the club, Eve, who was 'their high priestess'.

> I well remember my first entry into the dimly-lit room. It was draped with dark velvet curtains. There seemed to be a religious silence about the place; none spoke above a whisper. In the centre of the room there was a raised platform covered with black velvet, and there, beneath a brilliant spot light, stood a beautiful woman, her flesh glistening. There was a strange sacred feeling about the whole thing ... It was uncanny. There was no feeling or thought of sex. One was, as it were, transported to a different world where the lewd and suggestive were unknown.[7]

He captured the artists' models' limited liberation when he reflected:

> One night we made a discovery.
> We found that Eve never went away alone. A girl friend waited for her at the street door three storeys below, and they went home together. It was curious that she could well trust herself alone when stripped, but, when dressed, she was anxious to have the protection of another.[8]

It's an irony I know well. In the years after we separated, when Dan shattered the static to work abroad, I turned to art modelling to supplement a sporadic freelance income. It had become impossible to maintain a full-time job with Ruby on my own. She still needed domesticity; she drew comfort from consistency. I began after an idle comment from a friend who thought I belonged in a more bohemian age of history: 'I could imagine you as an artist's muse,' he said.

I made my way to the Julian Ashton Art School, founded in 1890 and known for its rollcall of famed artist graduates. If I was going to go nude, the artists better be good. My build was athletic from years of swimming rather than Rubenesque, but the artists didn't seem to mind. Afterwards I would, like George's Eve, wrap myself in the security of clothes to walk quickly among the crowds.

Perhaps on those nights when George was sketching his high priestess, Henry was home with Bertha, or on a binge with Victor Daley. Bertha mentioned the club briefly in 'Memories':

> They were a group of Bohemians – artists and writers – all poor. If they had money they shared it. If they had none, they would hold their meetings in a bar where they'd collect enough between them for a drink all round ... There were Bert Stevens and Fred Broomfield and Victor Daley and Fred Brown, the artist, and others. Harry took great delight in this congenial companionship, and very happy times they had together; particularly he loved Victor Daley, and until Victor died they were the closest and dearest of friends.[9]

Norman Lindsay blamed Henry for the reputation of the *Bulletin* staff as boozers. He said, annoyed:

> Seated in a railway train, I have heard myself described as a boozer of the first magnitude. Henry Lawson was mainly

responsible ... But all his best writing was done in the years of his comparative sobriety. Drunks do not create the basis of a national literature in prose and poetry ...[10]

In 1916, when attempting to secure a Commonwealth literary pension, Henry wrote to a Dr Watson, who was making enquiries into Henry's personal life. Hoping to improve his chances, Henry tried to rectify the club's reputation as 'a band of boozy, bar bumming bards'. He told Watson – imagine the doctor frowning as he read Henry's protests – that he and his *Bulletin* colleagues 'never drank to anything near the extent they gave us credit for'. Henry assured Watson that, even if they were drunkards, 'we were never blackguards and we never dealt in lies, false pretences, or dishonesty'.[11]

Names, dates, events and claims match and muddle together. Bertha said that, as soon as they arrived back from New Zealand, she was preoccupied with their baby and so she left the 'business affairs' to Henry. Their savings dwindled:

> It was here that I had my first experience of a bailiff – a stranger who knocked at the door and walked in. He sat in an easy chair and said he would wait, as he had plenty of time. When he explained he was a bailiff, put in on account of the rent, I was very distressed. Harry came home, sat down and had a yarn to him, took him out to have a drink, and I don't know what he did with him, but he never came back.[12]

For a time they moved in with Jack Lang and Bertha's sister, Hilda, at their home in Dulwich Hill. But Henry's binges soon strained the relationship with the in laws. Jack Lang recalled that one Friday evening, after he'd found Henry drunk with his mates, he'd taken Henry in a cab home to Dulwich Hill. But Henry, deciding the trip was too slow, was so obnoxious to the driver that Lang gagged him with a kerchief. Henry was unconscious when they arrived, and Lang thought he'd suffocated him. But to Lang's astonishment, Henry composed a new poem somewhere between being put into bed at home and Lang seeing him the next morning at the breakfast table.[13]

Dusker friend Fred Broomfield defended Lawson as a delight rather than a drunkard at this time, but they all seem equally drunk and delightful: 'he joyously took his place and his part among his fellows,' Broomfield proclaimed, and, rather than being a glum loner, Henry 'had humour, quaint and twisted'.[14]

For all his quaint, twisted humour, Henry was erratic in his work. One story, 'The Sex Problem Again', would later appear, reworked and edited, in anthologies of his work. It is obviously autobiographical and inspired by the continued tension in Henry's marriage:

> He loved her, and she loved him: but after they'd been married a while he found out that, although he understood her, she didn't and couldn't possibly ever understand him … But he couldn't leave her because he loved her, and because he knew that she loved him and would break her heart if he left her.[15]

Did he write it hungover after an argument when he'd once more stumbled home – tobacco juice on his jaw, beer on his breath, and a head that hurt as his wife snapped and shouted at the state of him?

In November 1898, Henry entered Rest Haven, on Sydney's tree-shaded North Shore. In an 1896 *Evening News* article, subtitled

'Sydney's Temperance Sanatorium for Male Inebriates: A Visitor's Impressions', an anonymous visitor wrote that the sanatorium had been established five years earlier, for the cure of inebriates and dipsomaniacs with an uncontrollable craving for alcohol.

The sanatorium was 'situated in one of the most picturesque and secluded recesses of Middle Harbor. For all practical purposes it is located as "far from the madding crowd's ignoble strife".' Rest Haven had orchards and gardens; the *Evening News*' visitor encountered 14 men, most of whom were 'gentlemen of education and culture':

> There is a clergyman in holy orders, a doctor, a musician, a veterinary surgeon, a squatter, two gentlemen of independent means, the brother of a leading solicitor, besides one or two literary men ... alcoholism is a nervous complaint, and often a concomitant of genius. It is rapidly coming to be recognised that the habitual abuse of stimulants is a disease, not a crime ...[16]

After six weeks of rehab, Henry, of nervous complaint concomitant with genius, emerged from Rest Haven and swore he would never drink again. Imagine Bertha holding him, thinking that they were now all the closer for the crisis that had beset them.

Henry wrote about his rehab in 'The Boozers' Home', in which he blurred himself as one of his favourite characters, Mitchell:

> Now, I'm not taking the case of a workman who goes on the spree on pay night and sweats the drink out of himself at work next day, nor a slum-bred brute who guzzles for the love of it; but a man with brains, who drinks to drown his intellect or his memory. He's generally a man under it all, and a sensitive, generous, gentle man with finer feelings as often as not. The best

and cleverest and whitest men in the world seem to take to drink mostly. It's an awful pity …

Now a drunkard seldom reforms at home, because he's always surrounded by the signs of the ruin and misery he has brought on the home; and the sight and thought of it sets him off again before he's had time to recover from the last spree. Then, again, the noblest wife in the world mostly goes the wrong way to work with a drunken husband – nearly everything she does is calculated to irritate him. If, for instance, he brings a bottle home from the pub, it shows that he wants to stay at home and not go back to the pub any more; but the first thing the wife does is to get hold of the bottle and plant it, or smash it before his eyes, and that maddens him in the state he is in then.[17]

Mitchell says that when relatives visited those who were in the boozers' home, it was 'pitiful':

It shook the patients up a lot, but I reckon it did 'em good. There were well-bred old lady mothers in black, and hard-working, haggard wives and loving daughters – and the expressions of sympathy and faith and hope in those women's faces! My old mate said it was enough in itself to make a man swear off drink for ever … Ah, God – what a world it is![18]

Imagine Bertha's face, expressing sympathy, faith and hope.

There's a photo of Bertha in a double-buttoned dress, as a new mother holding her baby son, alone and staring at the camera, in what is a predictive snapshot. There are Victorian studio photos of Henry, first as an excited young man, then frailer, but still with that distinctive moustache, and those large brown eyes that were inherited by his daughter.

And photos abound of Norman Lindsay's sketches of Archibald, of Lawson, and of Henry's Dawn and Dusk friends, Fred Broomfield and Victor Daley. A picture of an elegant George Robertson. Pinned together on a corkboard, they look like something from a crime-scene investigation.

But there's one more picture to add: that of the art model Hannah Thornburn. Fragments of her life remain in two of Henry's poems, 'Hannah Thomburn'[19] and 'To Hannah', and in a cryptic note from him many years later, asking Robertson to change brown eyes to grey in one of the verses of the first of these, adding, 'I wonder how I made that mistake? But I hadn't met my Grey Eyes then.'[20]

Mary Gilmore insisted to Henry's most prolific biographer, Colin Roderick, that Henry's poems about 'Ruth' are also Henry romanticising about Hannah.

There is a black-and-white photo of Hannah in Roderick's first biography of Henry, *The Real Henry Lawson*. Fair hair curls around her face and she raises her pointed chin. Her neck, half obscured by a collar, seems finely boned and long, as artists prefer. She looks away from the camera with a thoughtful gaze. She is softer than Louise Mack in the next photo. Louise, who contributed to *The Bulletin* when few women did, stares challengingly at the camera, daring it.[21]

The evidence that Hannah existed in Henry's life, Roderick asserts, lies in the unpublished memoir by Bertram Stevens, which detailed Hannah and Henry's friendship, if not something more. Stevens wrote:

The second child, Bertha, had been born in North Sydney a few months before they left for London (1900). I visited them several times around that time, & certainly thought the strain of sobriety was beginning to tell on Lawson. He found domestic affairs a burden & welcomed me as one upon who he could unload his troubles.

He had however found some solace in Hannah Thornburn. She was a rather delicate, plain girl, the daughter of a weak natured man who drank & was often out of employment. She was romantic: a poet of any kind would appeal to her & Lawson *the* Australian poet was regarded with something like worshipful admiration. She supplied the flattery & encouragement he did not get from his wife.[22]

Was Hannah flesh to Henry – a real relationship that arose out of his frustration with sobriety and family? Or a sweet siren, who was just a fantasy of Henry's, like those other, breasty models found in Norman Lindsay's paintings and Illingworth's sculptures, which are gazed upon by men imagining a different life? Henry's story 'The Sex Problem Again' may refer not just to tension in his marriage, but also to a conflict over whether to leave Bertha for Hannah.

Bertha and Hannah stare from the corkboard, capturing the state of Henry's mind.

There is a photo I can't find, of Ruby at five in her new school tunic that is too big for her, as all kindergarten children's are. In a blue folder, I unearth stuck-together baby shots glued by time: Ruby in my arms by an ocean pool days after she was born, my breasts still swollen; as a toddler cross-legged with a flower in the garden of our flat; in a merry-go-plane, at the zoo; at her bellydancing birthday party; and giggling in her frog swim-top beside me, pale in a bikini, smiling at her on the edge of a pool.

Memories melt together too, like her dad rushing to be at her first day of school, and meeting us, out of breath, by the demountable classroom. I can't remember where he was rushing from and I was hoping he'd be holding her hand in the photo I can't find. But perhaps that is the photo I want to see, as each trip away from Ruby and me had become longer. Six weeks, two months. Three months. The breaks in between were shorter. Our lives stretched across oceans. His was one of days at sea, strangers and shipshape order. Mine skidded between work and childcare as the house collapsed in the chaos of daily life.

When he was home, we existed in an atmosphere of restlessness, both loving Ruby but not sure if we loved each other as we once did. Trust was finely wrought like a wedding ring. It was enduring but, given a certain set of circumstances, it could quickly melt away.

Instead of the photo, I find postcards sent to us throughout 2004, her first school year, which I have kept for her. They are sent from Collioure, Port-Vendres, Positano, the Costa De Almeria, Venice. They all say the same thing: *I love you, I'll call.*

It's a consistency of sorts.

After Henry sobered up, the Lawsons moved across the harbour to the North Shore, which Bertha perhaps felt was further away from his bohemian club. She said that Henry was trying, always trying:

> For Harry was, above all things, loyal, affectionate, warm-hearted and deeply sincere. He was always greatly troubled at

our difficulties and with each decision that we made, each new venture that we tried, he would be as eager and excited as a boy. He would fling himself into it with immense energy and enthusiasm, and his discouragement would be profound when things did not turn out as we hoped they would.[23]

It was here in North Sydney that they met Mrs Byers, who would become integral to Henry's later life. 'It is just about twenty-one years since Henry Lawson came to my place, the North Sydney Coffee Palace,' Mrs Byers recalled.

> It was one Sunday afternoon, I remember, that he and his wife with the little baby, Jim – a baby in arms – came in and had afternoon tea. When they had gone out my little niece, who had waited on them, told me they had asked if we had furnished apartments to let. So my little niece ran after them and they came back and took a flat. I have often thought since how much is left to chance. But for the smartness of my niece in telling me and running after them and saying I would like to speak to them, I might never have known Henry Lawson ...
>
> I did not see very much of him except when he went in and out of the Coffee Palace and when he came to pay me at the end of the week for the flat. He always paid me in gold ... he was very much wrapped up in the works he was composing and was mostly writing.
>
> After a few months at 'the Palace', they left and took a cottage, not far from my place ... They were very busy in connection with their trip to England. This trip unfortunately for Henry brought him great trouble, some of the trouble I heard of while he was there, but many rumours were untrue, and Henry has told me of it since.[24]

Mrs Byers' ghost is sincere, and clear. She was more tolerant than Bertha, but then she didn't have a child and another pregnancy to contend with, which would have pushed Bertha's tolerance to exhaustion. There was a separation in Mrs Byers' past too, but perhaps like Henry's mother, Louisa, she could not quite face the ignominy of separation and divorce, which generated daily news in the papers. So, into the North Sydney cottage near the police station, a daughter, Barta (Bertha Louisa), was born in February 1900.

When Henry's intention to go to London was announced, the Duskers reunited for one last party together. They would also farewell English artist AH Fullwood, who was returning home to England around the same time. Fred Broomfield recounted:

> Bohemia in Sydney determined that the joint send-off should be a memorable one … On the April evening appointed for the great event, the gathering was so huge that it was by sheer good luck anyone escaped death by suffocation in the fierce struggle for admission.[25]

Broomfield wrote that the farewell, at the Victoria Cafe, ended with 'terrific midnight yells' at the ferry wharf, where Henry walked under a double arch of 'walking sticks, umbrellas, temporarily purloined palings, make-believe rapiers of ravished scantling, and arms raised skyward' onto a 'shriekingly impatient boat' to take him home to Bertha across the harbour.[26]

On 20 April 1900, the day of the sailing to England, the Duskers returned to wave off Henry once more. They stuffed a dashed-off poem from Victor Daley into the breast pocket of the captain of the *Damascus* and then 'adjourned to the Lord Nelson Hotel for five or ten minutes. Alack and well-a-day, we were there four and a half hours, awaiting the last siren of the *Damascus*; and, naturally, not a single soul of the whole company ever heard it.'[27]

Henry later wrote a poem about the send-off, 'For He Was a Jolly Good Fellow'. In the poem a woman stands apart from the whooping Duskers, her grey eyes staring at the boat:

> They cheered from cargo ways and ballast heap and pile,
> To last him all his days – they sent him off in style.
> (He only took his book.) He only turned his head
> In one last hopeless look towards a cargo shed
> Where one stood brimming eyed in silence by the wall –
> No jealous eyes espied that last farewell of all.[28]

The siren of London called.

The boat that was taking the Lawsons to London, the *Damascus*, stopped first in Melbourne, where Henry sat for John Longstaff in his Melbourne studio while the toddler, Jim, ran around the painter.

The portrait had been commissioned by *The Bulletin*. Henry wore the suit he had bought for London and fussed about the cuffs of his shirt, but Longstaff painted them out.

Henry recalled in 'The Longstaff Portrait':

> I was already a worshipper of John Longstaff because of his picture, 'Breaking the News'. I found him, as I'd vaguely expected, a big Australian – or rather Victorian (Gippsland, I think) – in every sense of the word ...

Longstaff quickly arranged 'the pose' (if I ever posed) and we had two or three hours at it, that morning. I think I could still watch that man work all day. I think it was the man I was watching rather than the artist ... Then at it again, after lunch ...

The sittings went on without interruption except once or twice; when Jim requested to be retired, and again, when he was making arrangements to fix himself comfortably for a quiet doss in the corner of the studio and got mixed up with a screen. He didn't complain even then. He was a quiet child ...

I had for years and have now – and I don't know how I got it – an idea that John Longstaff never knew that that picture was *finished*. He called it, 'a quick sketch in oils'. I've only seen it twice – once when it was wet and once when I returned from England in 1902. Perhaps the reason why I have never seen it since is that in a way, is that it is, in a way, connected with the tragedy of my life.[29]

On a visit to the Art Gallery NSW to see the Picasso exhibition, I'm accompanied by a reluctant Ruby. Afterwards, we wander around the rooms of Australian artworks, framed in elaborate gold to emphasise their importance. We pause in front of the Longstaff portrait. Henry looks dignified but excited. He's on the verge. London is calling.

'This is the writer I'm researching,' I explain to Ruby. I try to tell her about my writing, my work, to make it more tangible to her. 'His name is Henry Lawson.'

She scrutinises the picture: 'His moustache looks like a squirrel.'

Somewhere in the background, in Melbourne when Henry's portrait was being painted, there was Bertha and their second baby. Maybe she was visiting her brother. Or maybe she was rushing around buying essentials for the weeks at sea ahead. She said that the artist and Henry had to clean Jim up before he was brought back home to her, because the little boy was covered in paint.

She was anxious but excited too. Bertha recalled:

> Harry had a letter from Lord Beauchamp, then Governor of New South Wales, in October, 1899, asking him to call and see him. It was written after Lord Beauchamp had been on a trip outback. He had also read Harry's books and recognised his genius.
>
> He received Harry cordially and offered to pay our passages to England, so that Harry should win full recognition for his work. Without thinking of the difficulties of travelling with young children, Harry accepted the offer on the spot and came home radiant and jubilant, to think that at last he would get a firm foothold on the literary ladder.
>
> He laughed about my fears about travelling with a family, and we sailed in the 'Damascus' early in 1900, when my baby Bertha was only two months old, and duly arrived in London.[30]

5

Dated 30 July 1900, from Hertfordshire:

Dear Mother,

   I sat up nearly all night writing to you about a month ago, whether the letter was ever posted, we don't know. Harry can't remember posting it and I'm sure I didn't. For next day poor little Bertha was seriously ill with bronchitis and colic and for four days and nights I did not know what sleep meant … Jim is a shadow of himself, a poor miserable whining child. It is his teeth again, he is cutting his 2-year-old teeth together …

   I do hope they will be strong again before the cold weather sets in …

   We get very little time to feel lonely – but seldom talk of Sydney – for tears and lumps in my throat are my trouble and Harry is as miserable as a bandicoot for days. Oh I shall be glad when we can get back again. 'But we are not coming back hard up' and we are certain of success.

I don't like the climate a scrap – it's blazing hot one day and miserably cold the next. The winter is a real Bogey to us. How we are going to live through it I don't know. If Harry makes a splash we'll go to Italy or the South of France.

Dear Mother, I do wish you'll write soon. We crave for news from Australia … I do hope Hilda is over her trouble alright and that the newcomer is a son. Ask her to write too for I will write to her as soon as I can.

It's morning so I'd better get to bed. I wouldn't go to sleep until this was written or I would lose Wednesday's mail. If you should see any of our friends tell them we are getting on famously and Harry will write to all as soon as he gets this rush of work off …

Australia seems a dead world to the people here. There is no news in the English papers of it worth reading so if you can spare a paper occasionally we would be so thankful … If you should see Miss Scott [Sydney feminist Rose Scott] give her our kindest regards. I will write to her as soon as possible.

Give all our family my love. Love and best wishes to your own dear self.

Your affectionate daughter,

Bertha[1]

It's courageous of Bertha, moving so far so soon after her second child's birth. When Ruby's father and I went to London, we were still a just-married couple; we carried a backpack squashed with warm clothes rather than a baby in arms. Ruby would not be born until we returned from our year travelling and working in Europe. But Bertha had two, one just born. They were a family.

Henry wrote to George Robertson after the voyage, 'Wife and youngsters all right, but we had a hard time.'[2] The journey seems to have been difficult, even before they'd left the Australian coast. As they were departing Fremantle and entering Cockburn Sound, Henry managed to dash off one last letter to *The Australian Star*:

> Just going into the Sound. We go out in the morning, so I've just got time for a line. Beastly rough passage across the Bight. Captain McKilliam is a grand fellow; sticking to me like a toff. We are very comfortable. A great crowd on board, and oceans of 'copy' ... Have a large, four-berth cabin, plenty of room. The doctor is an old reader of mine – there are many of them aboard. Decent crowd. Good food. Kind regards to the boys. Goodbye, and God bless you all.
>
> Yours, all alive,
> Henry Lawson[3]

It was beastly, Bertha said, especially when they arrived in London. Although it was summer, she saw London through a 'grey drizzling mist'.[4] Initially they stayed in London with Nelson Illingworth's father, then, on the suggestion of their friend Edith Dean, they moved to Harpenden, a village north of London, which seemed more conducive to family life and less to drinking. Bertha tried to settle in once the children recovered from their bronchitis, and to adjust to the new surroundings and culture. The class-consciousness of the village was a shock after the bohemian political and literary circles of Sydney.

It seems that Bertha saw herself less as Henry's muse and more as his manager (with the agent JB Pinker in London to do the actual deals for his work). Or perhaps that's the image she wanted to portray, rather than the truth as she confided it to her mother in her letter. *Tell them we are getting on famously*, she instructed her mother to say if she saw their friends in Sydney. It was important to look respectable and affluent even when, behind the closed cottage door, it was a struggle. Fake it until you make it. We all do, don't we?

Bertha recalled:

> From our kitchen door we looked out over beautiful hayfields bordered with tall English trees. We loved to wander down the leafy lanes, and Harry was immensely interested in all the little farms, and in everything that was so different from far-away Australia and the bush. The little village was a haven of peace and comfort after our wanderings …
>
> It was delightful to live in a spot that was so happy and healthy for the babies, and we began to think that England was not the land of gloomy skies that had been painted.
>
> But, inevitably, Harry was drawn back into the life of London. His business necessarily took him into the city and he could not have avoided receptions and functions and the joyous meeting of old and new friends. And so Bohemia, with its trials and temptations, claimed him again.[5]

Later, she also wrote:

> This was calamity, for during the two years before we sailed for London, he had not touched liquor. His first slip was at the

farewell banquet given him in Sydney by his fellow writers and artists; and now, in London he fell again, disastrously.[6]

I receive an unexpected offer to visit London, where I can also research Bertha and Henry's time there. But I'm hesitant to leave Ruby; her dad is overseas too. After a decade of playing piano on cruise ships, he has settled in Los Angeles. Ruby's 20-year-old cousin offers to move in for the week to look after her. I am grateful for family yet again; they surround Ruby with security and support.

'Go,' Ruby urges. 'I'll be fine. Don't worry.'

I think about how she is used to one parent or both being on planes somewhere in the world. It feels like she is always left behind. Left for work, left for a date, left for a trip to London. Left by her dad.

I try to remember what I was like when Dan and I lived in London. I worked at 'Crumpet Tower' – the cabbies' nickname for IPC Magazines, because it was filled with women – and most days I was desperate for a walk on the Heath. We lived in a tiny attic flat above an off-licence shop that looked over rooftops, and I hunted around the lanes of Chinatown so I could make a Thai meal. I remember making friends, but never feeling at home. I have flashbacks of grasping strawberries and daisies on the first day of spring. Feeling the depth of the darkness in winter and sighing at its watery sky. Swimming at Hampstead Heath in summer, kicking cautiously in the bracken water, unable to shake my Australian fear that all brown water is dangerous because of what may lie beneath with teeth.

Spain was happier, when we visited Dan's father there. I remember arriving in the early hours at Benidorm, a beach town invaded by British tourists, and making love as the sounds of shrieks from the pool drifted into our room. I remember squinting because the sunlight was so bright in the taxi that sped beside orange groves into the country.

We stayed at a white villa, La Giraffe, where Dan's dad, an old bohemian pianist, and an artist friend spent much of the year. The plunge pool was shaded by olive groves, and the morning sun made long shadows on the terrace. We woke up warm and made love under a fan. It felt like home. Somewhere in a box there are photos of me smiling in a little blue denim dress. They are lost, like the past.

'What was I like in London?' I asked Dan before I got on the plane this time. 'I don't think it suited me. I was such a water baby.'

'We walked everywhere,' he said. 'And yeah, if you aren't used to it, the cold, and the early dark days … I think it got to you. You were so tired. You'd come home and want to go to bed. It was so long ago. God. Seventeen years.'

We share a history and a daughter. Divorce can't take that away.

6

Middlesex, Shepperton

Dearest Mother,

I was delighted to receive your letter. For I felt you had not forgotten me and glad you dropped it in the mud, for I now have a little bit of Sydney soil to cherish.

How sorry I am you have been kept in such suspense. Believe me, Harry did it out of kindness to your feelings.

Mother, I've been dreadfully ill, or else you would have had a letter from me, it is only within the last month that I've been able to write at all, and as you see I'm a little shaky still.

Do not blame Harry, whatever you do. He has been the best and most considerate Husband that ever lived and I were only half the good woman as he a man, I'd be self-satisfied. No, the fault was entirely mine. I have had too much responsibility for my years. You know what high pressure we had in Sydney, especially when Harry drank so heavily and then moving about so much, and the birth of the two little ones and the journey home [to England] finished me. An engine will only go a certain time and then will want repairing, and we mortals are the same.

Never mind, I fought the drink fiend successfully and have done other things that people twice my age would not attempt and I mean to fight this, the voices and all the other frightful nightmare of this disease, have vanished and I hope soon to be able to sleep naturally – I'm sick of sleeping draughts.

Now for something pleasant. Harry will make a big hit here, if only he keeps well physically. Oh, he has got so thin with the worry and trouble of this unfortunate illness. I expect to be soon home now and I'll fatten him up. Bertha has cut her teeth and Jim is in knickers though I have not seen him. Poor little mites, Harry has a kind, motherly old woman looking after everything but all the same it is not like a mother.

If Harry had been wise, he would have sent me to a Government institution instead of keeping me in a private place and paying three guineas a week for me …

Mother they drove me mad where I was before, well you understand more than I can tell you.

We had never heard of this beautiful hospital or I should have been here in the beginning. From the week I entered I've been feeling well. I expect to be home very shortly …[1]

There is no signature on this letter. It's dated 18 July 1900, but is thought to be actually from 1901. I'm not sure if there are final pages that have got lost or if Bertha just came to an abrupt, vulnerable end.

As the seasons changed, so did Bertha. She withered like the trees. She told her mother in a letter dated 11 September 1900:

> Everything is very dear, coal included ... I'm wretchedly lonely ... I'd give worlds to be back in Sydney. England is a grey, cold place. I'm sure we'll never get acclimatised and the weeks of grey sky are so depressing. We feel we are fighting a big battle and hope to come off successful ...

She signed off: 'I'm afraid I have the blues tonight.'[2]

Then she went quiet. Imagine her hunched in the cottage. I think of how soon after the birth of her second baby they left Sydney. The long, rough, 'dreadful' voyage. The English winter, after years of light and heat. Excitement of the new is gradually eroded by everyday living. Long summer days reduce to long dark mornings and nights. Children pale from bronchitis.

And for Bertha dreams become hallucinations.

Back in Sydney, in October 1900, Archibald also received a letter, from Bertha's friend Mrs Edith Dean, the Australian widow of the radical poet Francis Adams, who had been so keen to help the Lawsons on their arrival in England and had arranged for them to rent the cottage in Harpenden:

> Dear Mr Archibald,
> I know you will be dreadfully shocked to hear that poor Mrs Lawson has gone mad – driven so, I have no hesitation in saying, by her brutal husband. He has been drinking heavily and I quite expect the shock of him taking to drink again has

completely turned her brain

Three weeks ago my husband and I left home for a holiday leaving a servant here. On our return we find Mrs Lawson in the County Lunatic Asylum and Lawson in lodgings with my servant and the children in London ... I am troubled as to what Mrs Lawson is to do when she comes out. Do you know her mother's address. I believe too she has a brother in Melbourne who is well off and I wish you would let her people know – Lawson is such an unmitigated liar that I don't trust him ...[3]

Gossip travelled too, and it emerged in the papers, which Bertha's mother must have seen, or been told about, increasing her worry about her silent daughter. In the *Truth*, Maude Wheeler wrote in her expat column 'The Lights of London' on 28 April 1901:

And ever the singers, scribblers and painters come to inartistic London, and are lost in the vast maelstrom of her great dinginess. Poets and painters and fair young women all come, and all are swallowed up. Melba is the only one who has done any real good, the rest of them are nowhere. They fossick along in a dull uninteresting manner and long for Australia's blue skies, though they allow that they adore London and that its greyness is beauty. Pessimistic Lawson is here, buried in a dull, London flat, all alone. His wife craved and longed for the sunshine of her native Australia and is now in a mad-house, while her husband wanders about London and lives, nobody knows how. London calls![4]

Also, as Mrs Dean suggested, rumours were circulating that Henry had taken up with Mrs Dean's servant, Lizzie Humphrey, while

Bertha was locked away. But Lawson's flatmate at this time, the Australian poet Arthur Maquarie, defended Henry to Archibald and claimed that Mrs Dean was being malicious by implying Henry was the problem. 'While his name was being blackened to you, he and I were living quietly up the Thames,' Maquarie counter-wrote. As for Bertha, he added, 'her family are all shut up from time to time. There's fancy names for the malady but only one word for it – heredity.'[5]

The Bulletin also attempted to counter the gossip, reporting loyally that 'Lawson has had a terrible time (wife ill, &c.) and has come out of it like a strong man. He is doing well and has paid off the £200 advanced him by his literary agent during his wife's illness.'[6]

Allies bristle and defend. They clash over the facts. Locations jumped as Henry dealt with his family crisis: their son, Jim, was boarded with a lady in the village of Charlton, in Shepperton, Middlesex, not far from London and bordered by the Thames; Henry moved back to London into a flat with the servant, believed to be Mrs Dean's, Lizzie Humphrey, and with Maquarie (whom Mrs Dean calls a 'ne'er do well'), and, according to census records, baby Barta lived there too, at least initially. This makes sense, as Bertha was hospitalised in London. Then Henry returned to Charlton.

What also makes sense is that Henry would take a maid to help with the children. If he did have any relationship with the maligned Lizzie, it couldn't have been serious, because, unlike his romanticising of Bertha and Hannah, there's no legacy of lyrical poetry or prose idealising her existence, apart from a curious character reference to her in 'Triangles of Life'.[7] Lizzie washed away in the complicated story of Henry and Bertha, like the London rain they lived in.

Then, at some time in the following months, Henry moved to a cottage in the Shepperton area. It was from here that Bertha wrote her letters in 1901, just before and after she was discharged. It's messy and confusing, like all family crises involving mental illness are.

This much is clear: Bertha was first hospitalised in October 1900, at Bethnal House, London, just a month after she wrote from Harpenden to her mother, saying she had 'the blues'.

Bethnal House was advertised as 'a licensed house for the care and treatment of persons suffering from a mental disorder. Terms from 25s to £3.3 per week.'[8] In May 1901, Bertha was admitted for further treatment to Bethlem Royal Hospital at St George's Fields, London, where she was patient 2616. The 'mental disorder' was listed as lactation, and the person 'by whom authority sent' was recorded as 'Mr H. Lawson', with a deposit of ten pounds. Her period of treatment at these institutions lasted ten months, to August 1901, the following summer.[9]

Her initial admission notes at Bethlem in May 1901, recorded in its Register of Patients in black and red ink, state: 'Melancholia with ideas of unworthiness. Hallucination of hearing & suicidal tendencies.'[10] The certifying doctor recorded:

> She sat hiding her face in her hands and was most taciturn. She said 'I did it' over and over again, but would not state what. Stated she had no feeling anywhere, said she had killed both her children. Testimony by Florence Pope, a mental nurse in attendance at 123 Bond St London: tells me Mrs Lawson hears voices. Supposed nurse to be the devil. Unable to fix attention on anything. Her husband Henry Lawson tells me his wife attempted to get out of the upstairs window. Has begged him to kill her or give her the means to kill herself.[11]

Mother, she'd written, *I have the blues.*

Dated 2 November 1901:

Mother,

I'm writing to wish you all a very merry Christmas and a happy new year. Thank you very much for your loving letter, and don't worry about me, I mean to take care of myself in the future. We are all in splendid health but oh it is cold.

I'm writing by a blazing fire and have a thick jacket on and I'm still not warm. The fog is thick, you cannot see a dozen yards ahead. I do so sincerely hope this will be our last winter in England ...

Bertha and Jim are fat and roly. You would love the kiddies, they are so good. Jim is a very tall boy full of life and fun and Bertha is a pretty child. We'll get our photos taken as soon as we can afford it and I'll send one out. We were hoping we could send one to you [for Christmas].

It is still the same old struggle – but I think it will soon be over. Harry's new book will be out on the fifteenth. The country is looking desolate, all the leaves are falling and everything is bare, if we can raise the money we'll try and get to London for the winter. One would go melancholy here. I've had both children vaccinated last Thursday, small pox is raging and the authorities are waking up ...

Harry is truly fond of the children. He's been at it this afternoon making a train for Jim ...

How I wish we were spending Christmas together – we are lonely. I haven't a single friend. We never have a visitor, so unlike Sydney times.

We both feel sure of success but literary work goes slowly. I think after this year, the pinch will be over. Harry is fortunate in having a splendid agent, he charges ten percent but when I was ill he advanced Harry sixty pounds so he must feel confident of him and his work.

Dearest Mother, I wish you and Harry would meet, and I'm sure all the bitterness would be past. He never got the letter you wrote to Harpenden and kept putting off telling you the bad news in the hope there would be a change in my condition.

As far as the slander you heard was concerned, there was not a shade of truth in them – Harry is, and is doing all in his power to make me happy and to atone for the drinking days …

It is only sometimes I realise the distance between us and then my heart nearly aches in two. These are the days that make us homesick. Look out our front window and there's nothing but a thick sheet of fog through which you cannot see a yard, and go into the kitchen and it is full of clothes drying on the lines – I'm heartily sick of it – and the English are like their climate – as cold and as false as possible – and the talk of the war is sickening … London is rotten as far as society and politics go.

Dear Mother I shall have to say good night. Harry is waiting for the pen – again wishing you every joy and blessing for the New Year and with fondest love to you all from the family and

your loving daughter
Bertha

I'm not sending any cards this Christmas – can't afford it. I'll try my best to get our photos taken for you.[12]

The Bethlem Royal Hospital that Bertha knew is now the Imperial War Museum. The gardens, damp and green from perennial rain, teem with tourists photographing the naval guns and a segment of the Berlin Wall.

Inside, vintage fighter planes hang from the ceiling as marching songs and rolling newsreels blare commentary of battles and victory. I wasn't sure what to expect of this former asylum, given its notorious nickname 'Bedlam', which conjures up its older history of manacles and, in the late 18th century, 'lunatic baiting', which encouraged the sane to ogle the insane for a fee.

By the time Bertha was hospitalised in 1901, Bethlem practised dignity rather than tragedy-tourism, and straitjackets were removed upon admittance. The asylum had become a refuge for the middle class needing rest. A wall protected the patients' privacy. A minister of religion had to bear witness to mental illness before anyone could have their spouse or relatives admitted, to protect against claims of insanity that were really claims for inheritance or remarriage.

The windows are unchanged – large, with a view to the winter trees that are desolate and delicate like the patients who were once inside here. The galleries were decorated with ferns, birdcages, flowers and fishbowls: etchings of the hospital at the time depict women tending their needlework and cats curled up beside others with lost expressions on their faces. Residents ate meat, vegetables and pudding; the pharmaceutical remedies available included amyl nitrate for melancholy. Archival descriptions, recorded by writers who visited Bethlem in the late 19th and early 20th centuries, confirm Bertha's letters to her mother about her treatment.

Bertha's admission is highlighted now in a Bethlem heritage blog post about former patients who were relatives of famous people. She is listed alongside the mother of the artist JMW Turner and the niece of the slave-trader-turned-evangelist John Newton:

> Bethlem Hospital was relocated, reformed and changed beyond recognition in the course of the century that followed the admission of Mary Turner and Elizabeth Catlett. By 1904, the London *Argus* could opine that its arrangements were 'not so much those of an asylum or a hospital as of a first-class hotel'. Into this institution stepped a patient on transfer from the privately run Bethnal House in May 1901, one Bertha Lawson, then wife of the Australian poet Henry Lawson. The pair had come to London with their two young children in the hope that they could make their living by Henry's pen.[13]

The blog doesn't mention Bertha's escape attempt soon after admission, which Mary Gilmore recorded in her unpublished memoir and which she claimed was related to her in confidence:

> She had climbed a twenty-foot wall by means of a gas pipe, and reaching the Thames, started to swim across. A policeman, not knowing she was a good swimmer, jumped in to save her. He could not swim and she nearly drowned him. He contracted pneumonia and Henry had to pay his expenses besides giving him five pound for saving his wife.[14]

Imagine Bertha making strong, sure and swift strokes in the river, with the cold current shocking her senses. Was she having a psychotic episode at the time, seeing a too-bright sky and gas lamps on the bank glowing like fireballs? Or perhaps she was frightened, but sure of her sanity? Was she swimming to the opposite shore – to her children, or to Australia?

Imagine her struggling with the brave, weaker policeman, him forgetting propriety and grabbing her around her waist, her breasts, her legs, anywhere to keep hold of her thrashing body, shouting for help. Someone must have come, or Bertha must have given up, because she returned to Bethlem and became a quiet, lost face.

Mother, I've been dreadfully ill.

In 'Memories', Bertha mentioned her illness but did not disclose her swim in the Thames that Henry allegedly told Mary Gilmore about at the time. Perhaps it's to be expected: there's still a stigma attached to mental illness now, let alone 100 years ago.

She wrote instead:

> To add to our troubles I became very ill, suffering badly from insomnia which ended in a complete breakdown. For months I was in hospital, the home was broken up, and the babies were boarded with a Mrs Brandt at Charlton, a little village near the Thames. Harry had been frantically distressed about my illness, and now he worked manfully, keeping quite right and devoting himself to looking after me and helping to nurse me back to convalescence. As I grew stronger we were very happy again. For, save in those dark moods for which he was not really responsible, Harry was a wonderful companion – sensitive, keenly appreciative, and very kindly. I know how grateful he always was, how firmly determined never to fail me again, and how hard he battled, through all the years, against the almost insurmountable difficulties of deafness, nervousness, poverty,

discouragement, and ever-present temptation. That highly nervous temperament of his, which caused his moods, had also endowed him with a great vitality and a power of feeling and understanding which carried him through the dark places of his life, leaving the bitterness behind.[15]

On a drizzling, misty morning the North London bus drives past housing estates and graffitied sports fields. There's no Georgian grandeur here, just streets that are drab and damp. Washing that will never dry hangs on balconies; cheap lace curtains line the windows of bland brown brick terraces. A man shuffles to the disability centre as another yells to the rain. Pigeons flock around the corner of the park and mothers push strollers covered in plastic to the play centre. More brown units obscure the view of the park. At the back of the play centre is Paradise Row, the lane in which Henry and Bertha lived during their last months in London. Bertha wrote that they were squashed by poverty:

> Matters went from bad to worse. Our cottage at Harpenden had to be given up. We took an attic flat of two small rooms and a kitchenette and bathroom in Paradise Lane, off James Street and Holloway Road. Here I had Harry under my eye …[16]

Overgrown fences back onto the Row, separating aged, white buildings that look to have never changed. But who really knows, in a city that changes all the time? One fence gate opens onto a building site. The lane is much prettier and more private than the other streets around here. There's no 'Henry Lived Here' blue plaque from London Heritage, like on the homes of many other writers who lived in London. But, compared to the neighbourhood, it is paradise.

A tube stop away is Gray's Inn Road, where Henry apparently stayed with his 'ne'er do well' friend Arthur Maquarie, the servant Lizzie Humphrey and his baby daughter in Clovelly Mansions. Today it is London live – a hub of shops, traffic and people.

Henry would have felt comfortable here. A London local. 'A literary lion', as Bertha called him. Charles Dickens' museum is around the corner; and next to a sprawling, modern silver office building, mansion apartments still stand like an elegant old lady.

In this search for ghosts, the name Clovelly Mansions has mostly vanished, apart from references to Katherine Mansfield, the New Zealand–born short story writer, living there a decade later in 1911.

At the local library I ask about the Mansions. They're close to Bloomsbury: it seems Henry was edging towards literary London.

'Was it fashionable to live here?' I ask. 'Or grungy?'

'More grungy,' the librarian replies. 'It's not Virginia Woolf …'

'Dodgy Bloomsbury?' I offer.

'Yes,' he says.

7

To David Scott Mitchell, 11 February 1902, written from the office of literary agent JB Pinker at Effingham House, Arundel Street, Strand, London:

Dear Mr Mitchell,

Have had a very bad time since I wrote last, and Mrs Lawson has had a very long and severe illness – however, things look bright again …

It takes about two years' good work to get a footing in London – but *good work will go* in the end. I expect to be well on my feet this year and hope to take Mrs Lawson out to Australia before next winter. But of course I'll return to London …

I have three or four publishers after me now and would have been in a comfortable position but for the heavy expenses of Mrs Lawson's illness …

Of course I've heard all about the cowardly stories that were circulated concerning me in Sydney. The origin of those lies is

too paltry and contemptible for me to explain. I dare say Miss
Scott knows the truth by this time. These are lies that a man
cannot fight. But I might tell *you* some things some day. But
what does it matter? ...

Mrs Lawson and children are blooming. Please remember
me to Miss Scott. I heard she was one of the few friends who
remained true to me.

Trusting to see you by next Christmas,

Yours ever gratefully,
Henry Lawson[1]

Apart from her brisk disclosure of her breakdown in 'Memories',
Bertha offers few clues about her state of mind. Her voice in *My
Henry Lawson* is calm, confident and controlled. It has the same
tone as that in the letter to her mother once she was recovering.

As she had anticipated, after she was discharged from Bethlem
she joined Henry and the children in Shepperton. They then moved
back to London for the winter and took the small flat, up five
flights of stairs, in Paradise Row. Lizzie had disappeared except for
Bertha's reference to rumours in her letter to her mother: 'As far as
the slander you heard was concerned, there was not a shade of truth
in them.'[2] The stories had circulated all the way around the globe to
Australia and back to Bertha in London.

In spring 1902, London was warming up, but there were still
late frosts. Mary Gilmore wrote to Henry with the news that she,
together with her husband, Will, and their son, Billy, were in
Liverpool; they were en route from Paraguay to Sydney. Henry and
Bertha urged them to stay at their London flat.

The spring frosts reflected the atmosphere that quickly developed in the flat between Mary and Bertha, who had never previously met before. Twenty years later, Mary recollected this time in her unpublished mini-memoir, 'Personal History: Henry Lawson and I'. Reading it, I can see why it wasn't published at the time, why Mary marked it 'personal and private'.[3] Bertha would have sued.

> When we arrived at the flat it was a little earlier in the day than Mrs Lawson expected. Her hair was not done as she usually does it and she was only just tidying up. The first thing that struck me was the thickness of her neck, and the wedge-shaped frontal part of her head. The forehead sloped back at the top and at the sides. The combination of [her] thick neck and narrowed top to the intellectual part of the head struck me as strange and gave me a sense of dismay. But she was cordial (Henry had just gone out) and in the excitement of meeting, the feeling passed. She made us a cup of tea and told us that she had been longing for a chance to get back to Australia and her mother and that when my letter reached them it had been decided at once that here was the chance. She also asked that we should not let Henry know she had told of her wish to go with us to Australia as he would mention it himself.[4]

Bertha gave Mary and her family the only bedroom in the tiny flat. Bugs fell from the ceiling at night onto the bed and Mary jabbed them with her umbrella when they scattered at the first spark of light. Drunken fights in the streets outside disturbed the nights.

To eat, Mary described:

> At tea time later on I sat on a box with my back against the sink, Lawson sat in a deck chair at the opposite end of the

table, my husband next to him on the only strong four legged chair. Lawson was still paying off the bills for the Asylums for the Insane where his wife had been for months and so was very poor. The table could not be moved from the wall as Will and Mrs Lawson would have their backs roasted against the stove.[5]

There was no bathroom, so they washed themselves in a tub in the communal laundry. She noticed that in other flats there were children who were locked up all day while their mothers went to work.

Mary was obviously uncomfortable in the Dickensian surroundings that Henry, Bertha and their two children lived in. But she said she was more disturbed by Bertha's claims that Henry was abusing her; Bertha's confidences about her marital unhappiness began 'within half an hour' of their arrival.

'Bertha said that nothing on earth would make her live with him again once she got away,' Mary recalled.

She continued to talk of her relief at our coming and the release of getting 'home' to her mother. Her use of the word 'home' confusing me, I said once, what place did she really mean by 'home'. She said, 'where my mother is. When I get back to her I shall never leave her again'.

Again and again she told me that she 'hated' Henry and that once she got away she would never return to him. 'He thinks I will come back and I do not say anything, but he is mistaken,' she said. I never met anyone express hatred so vindictively as she did.

The next day the two men went out after breakfast and did London parks. After tea, the men disappeared. That day Mrs

Lawson still told of her miseries with Henry. But I had begun to doubt her and said that Henry seemed fond of her and the children and that nothing unkind showed in his manner. 'That is his cunning,' she said. 'That is all put on!' ... She also told me he had tried to kill her with a carving knife.[6]

But Mary said she could see 'no visible scars'.[7]

Mary's husband, the adventurer and farmer she had met at the New Australia settlement in Paraguay, intensely disliked 'Mrs Lawson'; first of all for openly telling them about her marriage, and then more so after hearing what Henry confided in him man to man as they walked around London. The microfilm containing her memoir is a Pandora's box:

That night, Will told me Henry had told him the story of the Asylum, Mrs Lawson's false charges against him, in regard to the servant etc. and all the trouble he had had. And my husband said he did not believe a word Mrs Lawson said, that he was sure she cared nothing for Henry, only for what she could get out of him; that in his opinion she had only married him for his name and position, and that having no position in London, she wanted to get back to Australia where she could be somebody as Mrs Lawson. He said he pitied Henry and would take his least word where he would not take Mrs Lawson's oath ...

I could feel my husband's antipathy had increased as a result of the morning talk with Henry. Also he did not like her loud and vulgar manner when in the theatre. That night he said, 'If that woman were my wife I would wring her neck! She isn't fit to be any man's wife.'[8]

According to Mary, Will's view was confirmed when they met Nelson Illingworth's father in London, with whom the Lawsons had initially stayed when they came to the city, and who told them: 'She [Bertha] was only suited to a man who would stand no nonsense but who would knock her down when she "tried on her games".'[9]

Will was furious when he heard Bertha whispering to Jim about Henry, 'He's a bad man,' just quietly enough so that Henry, half-deaf, couldn't hear.

> It was this kind of thing that used to make my husband say if she were his wife he would wring her neck. And once (for he is not that kind of man) 'There is only one kind of thing that sort of woman understands and that is the fist'.[10]

Mary claimed that Henry originally intended to stay on in London for six months or so at least after Bertha left, so he could work away from his wife and take his place in literary history, and that he had no intention of coming back to Australia soon. She decided that Henry's unhappiness was because of 'the injustices heaped upon him' and claimed that Bertha confided to her that she sometimes threatened to throw the children out the window if Henry did not do what she wanted. Mary continued that Bertha's doctors at the hospital 'spoke of Henry in the highest possible terms'.[11] She said Henry was so anxious about the children's welfare that he did not want Bertha and the children to travel alone to Australia, so he was very thankful that Mary and Will were accompanying them on the long voyage. Mary wrote that Henry, always the poet, told Bertha, 'you are not mad Bertha, but bad'.[12]

Or was Mary exaggerating, to provide evidence for her own portrait of Bertha as 'not mad, but bad' and so the principal cause of Henry's woes? Mary said she checked with Bertha's doctor in London prior to their voyage to Australia and he told her that he sympathised with Bertha, 'as any woman was to be pitied who had a husband who drinks'. He recommended that Bertha return to Australia for at least six months.[13]

But Randolph Bedford, another Australian writer living in London, visited the Lawsons in their paradise slum, and later wrote it was Henry who wanted to return:

> I went to see a friend – an Australian writer who has made a bigger stir in Australia, where his work is known and rewarded, than he ever will here. He lives beyond Islington, and curses England, crying to be delivered from the body of this death and to be set down in an Australian sun again. If ever he says a good word of the country it will be from sheer perversity.[14]

Truth, claims and memory pace around each other.

Before leaving for London, I saw a lady admiring a collection of Swarovski jewellery on display in a vintage accessories shop.

'I have a lot of it,' the shop owner told the customer. 'People see it and say, "I have something," and bring it in.' This was a tiny shop, an open conversation.

'I have a Swarovski tennis bracelet,' I agreed. 'It was a guilt present my ex gave me.'

'I'll sell it for you,' she offered. 'You don't need to hold on to his guilt.'

Soon after, in London, returning on the bus from the War Museum to the city centre and surrounded by landmarks, I had another flashback: it was here in London that Dan had given me the tennis bracelet that the shop owner suggested I sell. Just before our divorce, Dan and I planned to meet in Paris. A romantic reunion after yet another three months apart. My mother, who lived an hour's flight away from Sydney, vehemently disapproved of Dan's extended separations from us and took Ruby home to her beachside town for the time I would be away. 'This is rough. You need a break,' she insisted. I'd stopped defending him.

We reunited in London – him flying in from a cruise and me from Australia – and he gave me the narrow blue box, embossed with the Swarovski name and containing the bracelet. He pressed it into my hand and seemed awkward. The next day we caught the Eurostar to Paris, the bracelet wrapped around my wrist.

It is really a forgotten memory of disunion. You imagine reunions will be a surge of heart, a restorative hug – affirmation that being together again reveals how much you missed each other. But reunions aren't always as they are imagined. They often mark the end rather than another beginning, and remembered details then blur in the tears of the time.

'I have another cruise,' Dan said, as we stood on a bridge looking at the Seine.

'How long?' I asked.

'Six months.'

My sense of solitude over the last year had been emotional as much as physical: the space in my bed, but none in my life; the sporadic phone calls that only emphasised how apart we were; and, most of all, the child who grew a little more every day without her father, who chose not to be there.

I didn't cry. Maybe it was because the end had been such a long time coming, or because I had for too long now been sleeping alone and caring for our child by myself. Or, I had already cried too many times before this day in Paris.

'I want a divorce,' I said.

The liner *Karlsruhe* had two masts, was constructed of steel and steamed at 13 knots. There were 44 cabins in first class, 36 in second and 1955 in third, or steerage. In April 1902, William Gilmore, Mary, their son, Billy, and Bertha and her two children were among the throng below deck. During its 35-day trip to Australia, the ship was on an incidental world tour, carving a route via Genoa, Cairo, the Suez Canal, Aden, Bombay and Colombo, and then across the Indian Ocean to Fremantle, around the Bight to Adelaide, Melbourne and finally Sydney.

On the day of departure, Henry had intended to accompany the little party on the train to the dock. But tension between Henry and Bertha soured the farewell, Mary said. A fight between them had begun the day before, when Henry was supposed to pick up the money for the tickets from his agent, Pinker: they had argued about whether he should go alone and this sparked a 'fearful row':

> She told him she had always hated him, that she hoped she would never see him again once she got away and that not even if she was dying would she come to him again ... Henry was sad for the trouble, sad for the parting, anxious beyond belief for the children, and half afraid that he was putting too much risk on us in putting her in our charge. His wife showed neither grief nor anxiety. Her one idea was to get away ...

She would not have Henry come to the ship, so they parted at the train. She neither shook hands with him nor kissed him. She crossed to the side of the carriage farthest from him, turned her back on him and drew the children's attention from their father to the scenery. He stood sad and humiliated at the other window.

'Aren't you going to say goodbye, Bertha? You are going to the other side of the world and we may never see each other again,' he said ...

My husband said to me, 'did you ever see anything so callous in all your life? She even prevented Jim from saying goodbye to his father.' And so we set out on our journey.[15]

Whoever was spinning, the truth of it was that Mary, at Henry's request, was reluctantly escorting his wife home, believing the only cause of Bertha's breakdown had been Bertha herself.

Her opinion of Bertha worsened on the ship: she says Bertha shocked other passengers by asking for an eye-glass when, in Egypt, a nude local rushed along the bank beside the ship. She flirted with staff. Sightseeing in Genoa, Mary claimed, Bertha in a temper appalled Italians at the Campo Santo fountain by hitting Jim with his own fist, blacking his eye.

In Mary's memoir, the growing tension between the two women builds like the waves crashing against the ship:

It had been arranged by Henry that I was to write at each Port and let him know how things went, for he was afraid of the insanity, and terribly anxious for the children ... He was very sad and there was a pleading note in his voice that brought the tears to my eyes ...

I was so upset over her rage in the Campo Santo, Genoa that when I got back to the ship I wrote a full account of everything for posting at the next port of call ...

Henry, fearful for the children's mental inheritance, lest it should be unstable, had asked me to write a full account of them and my opinion of them after I should be at sea. At Aden I did this, saying exactly what I thought of them as to appearance, capacity, and futures. Jim, I said, was like Henry, and from his highly strung sensitive temperament I expected him to be a writer or an artist. Bertha [Barta] I regarded as more like her mother, and that she might possibly make a successful and cheap and popular novel writer ...

The letter I last mentioned I took along and posted. About an hour later I went up on deck. I noticed a crowd of people and Mrs Lawson amongst them. As soon as she saw me she rushed at me and struck me shrieking, 'I'll teach you to write to my husband behind my back!' and indulged in a series of accusations and charges in the most vulgar and violent language ...

As I saw that she had my letter in her hand I said, 'since you have stolen my letter, and since you have made accusations before all these people, I insist on you reading that letter aloud so that the people who have heard you will know just what I have written.' She refused ...

I ordered her to read what was written ... The passengers turned away saying 'Well there is nothing in <u>that</u> letter to make a fuss over!' I took the letter from her, and too put out to realise that I should meet vindictive cunning with care, tore it up and threw it into the sea.[16]

By June 1902, the *Karlsruhe* was moored in the spiced heat of Colombo harbour after 'a series of misfortunes'.[17] It had lost a propeller blade due to floating wreckage, then encountered the tail of a cyclone, mirroring the rough passage on board between Bertha and Mary. In Colombo, they reluctantly came together on deck looking out for Henry, who was due to join them any day. He'd sent a telegraph to let them know he'd left London on the next ship bound for Australia, after he'd completed the proofs of his book *The Children of the Bush*, and finalised the practicalities of their London life.

Mary maintained that she stopped writing to him after the letter fight on the deck, but that he feared for the children and gave up his London career to be with them. Henry always said he delayed his passage because of the *Children of the Bush* final edit.

It was a toxic triangle. Reflecting on the 'long-established rumour' that Mary Gilmore and Henry had the affair Bertha had suspected when she confronted Mary over the letter, their friend Ruth Park later wrote in her memoir *Fishing in the Styx*: 'My personal opinion is that the "love affair" was one of Henry's little brags with which he successfully wounded his estranged wife. The tale possibly wounded Mary Gilmore also. But the truth will probably never emerge from the shadows of the long gone past.'[18]

In Colombo a catamaran neared the *Karlsruhe*. As it drew closer, Bertha saw a figure,

> white-clad from hat to shoes, standing in the bow, while the crew salaamed to him as if he were a prince. Piled on the outrigger were heaps of oranges, guavas, durians and other kinds of fruit, all belonging to Harry, it proved. For needless to say the

tall, gaunt figure in white was he — but it was a Harry who had celebrated well.[19]

Imagine Mary Gilmore smiling and Bertha's mouth becoming set as he boarded with his booty. Bertha recalled that her husband was contrite, but 'I still felt hurt and could not forgive him'.[20]

They sailed for Sydney, and separation.

8

'To Hannah', first published in *The Bulletin* in 1904:

> Spirit Girl to whom 'twas given
>> To revisit scenes of pain,
> From the hell I thought was Heaven
>> You have lifted me again
> Through the world that I inherit,
>> Where I loved her ere she died,
> I am walking with the spirit
>> Of a dead girl by my side.
>
> Through my old possessions only
>> For a very little while,
> And they say I am lonely,
>> And they pity, but I smile:
> For the brighter side has won me
>> By the calmness that it brings,

And the peace that is upon me
    Does not come of earthly things.

Spirit girl, the good is in me
    But the flesh you know is weak
And with no pure soul to win me
    I might miss the path I seek;
Lead me by the love you bore me
    When you trod the earth with me,
Till the light is clear before me
    And my spirit too is free.[1]

On board the *Karlsruhe*, Henry's mood rotted like the fruit he'd flamboyantly carried aboard. As soon as he changed ships, he said, the voyage home went from heaven to hell. But Mary was 'too thankful for words' that Henry had arrived to take charge of his wife.[2] Mary had decided Bertha was still certifiable.

Imagine the oceanic arguments between Henry and Bertha, their tempers pitching like the sea they sailed across, until Henry jumped ship in Adelaide in July 1902, leaving Bertha and their children on board once again.

I reach back into my own memories. I remember Dan – 'You don't mean it,' he'd said on the Eurostar. 'We'll talk about it.' I flew back to Sydney alone.

'Oh love,' my mother said, reliving her own divorce. 'Do you think he'll come back?' She had a picture of us in a frame on her dresser, taken soon after we met, our arms wrapped around each other, in black t-shirts. Now she moved a book in front of Dan's face.

Then, a few days later, he flew back too. Ruby flung herself at him as he came in, and clung to him. He produced a world of presents bought in ports everywhere, including a Russian doll with wolf hair and an exotic Barbie in a sari. Ruby placed them beside her pictures of him – one of him playing the piano and one of him with her as a baby. It was a little shrine to him, the life she remembered – the life she wanted back.

While Ruby slept, he said, 'I'm going to do this cruise. I think we should have a break. I don't want to be a sad old fuck in a shop. I want to have my career and I can't have it here. I'm going to miss seeing her grow up … this is the hardest thing I've had to do.'

There are no photos of our split, of Dan's hug and a kiss for Ruby on the stairs by the frangipani tree shading the apartment windows, as the taxi waited on the street. Of Ruby's resigned, sad face as we said goodbye again. Ruby's hand in mine as the taxi sped away to the airport, away from us.

Bertha had a version of Henry's flight and Mary Gilmore had her story, derived partly from her memory of events and partly from Henry's confidences. It's as though the two women are whispering in each of your ears.

Bertha's story blamed her outrage over Henry's fruit- and alcohol-laden arrival onto the ship in Colombo Harbour for making the voyage tense. She wrote:

> Harry left the ship at Adelaide and travelled to Melbourne by train, in order to interview my brother and ask him to arrange a reconciliation between us. Eventually this was done there, at a family dinner at my brother's home in Williamstown.

Harry and I had twenty four hours together in Melbourne.
Then he set off again by rail, to prepare a home for us in
Sydney ... However, I stayed with my mother for six weeks,
when we set up house-keeping in a house at Manly.[3]

But Mary Gilmore implied that Henry sailed all the way to
Melbourne, where he had another reconciliation in his heart and
mind. With a love letter in his pocket, he rushed to meet the
Bohemian girl who had moved to Melbourne while he'd been in
London. Mary called the girl 'Ruth', though this was Hannah.

Here also he had gone out hoping to see 'Ruth'. He came
back broken-hearted. Ruth was dead. She had left him a little
message of love – her unforgettable love and understanding. I
think Ruth must have been a second Mrs Byers only young, and
fresh with the sweetness of youth. Lawson had told me all about
Ruth. Once she said to him, 'I would like to have a child to
you Harry ... I would like to be the mother of your child. How
wonderful he would be.'

When he went ashore at Port Melbourne he told me, 'If I
can only find Ruth and lay my head in her lap I will be cured of
all my trouble.' He had told Will about Ruth, too. Sometimes
I think Ruth must have died in actual childbirth, but I do not
know. I was so sorry for Henry that I could have told him
to lay his head in my lap; only that when you are married to
someone else you do not do these things.[4]

The last time Henry had been in Melbourne was two years earlier,
when he had sat for his portrait in Longstaff's studio, alight with
expectation for success in London. Today, trams still roll past that

studio building, crammed with commuters, iPhones instead of letters in their pockets.

In a letter to George Robertson, Mary wrote:

> As long as I live I shall never forget that little bit of soiled and crumpled paper, which had never left that man's pocket – the breast pocket – and which held a hope that kept him able to endure. I have heard many men's stories, many stories of men and women, but none so tragic as this; and this one I *saw*, for he showed me the slip with a face alight as he left the ship at Williamstown, and he came back to me with the light quenched and his life in ashes.[5]

He was six weeks too late.

Little is known of what happened to Hannah Thornburn, beyond brisk medical details and what Henry confided to Mary Gilmore on that day on the ship.

She had been living in Melbourne and working for her parents at their music store. But on 1 June 1902, aged 25, she was taken to hospital, where she died two days later at 2.30 am from 'endometritis' according to her death certificate – or, as Colin Roderick primly explains in a 1968 article about her, 'inflammation of certain internal reproductive organs'. He means those scary women's bits he couldn't bear to utter: the uterus, the fallopian tubes and the cervix. Such primness is absurdly confusing.

However, Roderick's research into Henry's mystery girl discovered more about her death than is known about her life. His 1968 article continues:

When Hannah was admitted to hospital she declared herself to be a 'domestic' and to be four months pregnant ... She had been troubled for a fortnight and had seemingly been in a serious plight for a week. As the weekend wore on she grew weaker; her temperature rose, her pulse fell, and death supervened at half-past two o'clock on the Sunday morning.[6]

In his Lawson biography, published in 1991, Roderick is still prim, but braver in discussing the finer details. He adds Hannah was

four months pregnant and about a fortnight earlier had been taken ill on a railway station. She said three or four days later while at stool something had come away. Four days before admittance she'd lost a clot of blood and began douching herself ... Within twenty-four hours of admittance her temperature had soared and a curette became mandatory. The size of the foul placental mass that this yielded indicated Hannah had left it too late to effect a recovery from the septic condition of her reproductive organs. Her condition worsened during the night, her pulse weakened, and she died early next morning ...[7]

Now it makes sense. In 1902, 'endometritis' could have been an official euphemism for a very unofficial botched attempted abortion.

Imagine Mary Gilmore consoling Henry on the ship in Melbourne when he returned. His 'life in ashes', as Mary dramatically wrote.[8] Ashes to ashes, dust to dust – the funeral rite would have been intoned over Hannah's casket as it was lowered into a YMCA shared grave in a Melbourne cemetery, six weeks earlier.

9

Handwritten letter, undated but probably early August 1902, from Bertha Lawson to Henry Lawson, who was resting in what was referred to as 'Nurse Keys' Private Hospital':

3 Beauchamp Terrace
Whistler Street,
Manly, Friday

I've got no paper, so I'm going to write on this. I won't come in tomorrow, it is such an expense it cost me 2/6 last night. I'll bring the children in early on Monday. And we will spend the day with you. I'm so glad you are getting on so well. We will be very happy yet. You must just let your own good nature overcome the evil one. Six months won't be long skipping past. And I'll come and spend one day a week with you. You must make great resolutions for the future and you will keep them, I know. Above all get to work and work hard. By so doing, you will forget the past and you will also forget yourself in your work. And I want you to make the most of your chances. You know you are a long way ahead of all Australian writers. But every week you let go by is so much lost. And it makes way for others; get ahead with your novel. It will be a big success and you must sell your work now, because your name is now before the public on account of C[hildren] of the Bush. You know dearie, in the past you have always let your opportunities slip past. Be like Kipling now, and make the most of it. We are always growing older never younger. And I never think a writer writes such good work after he is fifty years old.

So now work hard and you'll be happy. Jim is not very well. He is so troubled so with worms. I'm giving him a treatment for them. I think I'll take him to the Dr tonight. These bills have been worrying me greatly they keep asking me for them. So Dearie I'll be glad if you can fix them up. We have a good name here as far as debts are concerned. I've paid the rent and 7/6 for vegetables. And I really can't pay any more. There is a bill for bread for 9/- to Harper. I've paid the other bread bill myself.

Goodbye till Monday.

With love from the youngsters and your wife.
Bertha Lawson[1]

In July 1902, far from the streets of Darlinghurst, Henry heard the clattering of train wheels over tracks as he travelled ahead from Melbourne to Sydney. Imagine his head against the train window as it travelled north, past rain and dust. Imagine, too, his wife and children aboard the ship as it steamed to Sydney, feeling the winter southerly blow across the decks and the chill of an uncertain future.

When Bertha arrived in Sydney, Henry was resting at a convalescence hospital at the urging of Archibald, who said, 'Lawson is suffering much from nerve trouble.' He was cheerful upon release, writing to his friend, theatre producer Bland Holt: 'Went into a private hospital for a spell, where there were six pretty nurses and I the only good-looking patient. Was getting very contented when Mrs Lawson called and fetched me home.' He added, 'She is blossoming into an authoress.'[2]

Bertha seems to have softened. A reunion had taken place. Why do we reunite, though, when we know it is ending? Perhaps we do it for the children. Perhaps we reunite because a separation is so daunting, so overwhelming, that it is easier to try again with promises whispered in bed. Bertha never revealed if she knew Henry was trying to leave the marriage as well as the ship in Melbourne. Perhaps she knew that a certain Bohemian girl was gone for good. That part of Henry's life was in ashes.

She seems tired in her letter to him at the hospital, written after she arrived in Sydney Harbour. She was only 25, dealing with two small children – Jim was four; Barta, two – as well as mounting bills and an alcoholic husband with frustratingly great promise, if only he'd pick up a pen more often than a beer. 'You've got your name before the public now,' she urged. 'Work on your novel. Be like Kipling.'

When Henry was discharged, they lived in small cottages – 'Beauchamp Terrace', 'Marlow' and 'Ladywood', a few streets back from the harbour and Manly Beach, whose slogan was 'seven miles from Sydney and a thousand miles from care'.[3] Imagine them strolling along the beachfront on the winter sand, making plans, once more, for the future.

But as summer came, stress spiralled again. This time they couldn't blame the lack of sunshine, because it was glaring through the windows. Hear the shouts drifting on the sea breeze as the children sleep in their rooms. Then they have no beds to sleep on, because the furniture is seized in lieu of rent. Imagine Bertha hunched over with worry, as she was in the cottage in England. Henry misread her anxiety as being 'insane' and confided so to Bland Holt. He asked for money: 'I will have £50 on December 1st. She is the mother of my children and therefore—'[4]

The letter stops. It's a scrawl for help. He blames her mental state. She blames poverty, and his drinking. We always blame each other.

We will be happy yet.

Some letters are written from the heart, in recognition of a failing marriage. Yet some letters, equally personal in nature, are flat and fearsome. On 6 December, the Metropolitan Police District in the State of New South Wales summoned Henry to the Water Police Office, Sydney:

> Whereas ~~information~~ complaint on oath hath this day been made before the undersigned, one of His Majesty's Justices of the Peace in and for the said state of New South Wales for that ~~you did~~ on the fourth day of December at Manly in the said District Bertha Marie Louise Lawson was compelled under reasonable apprehension of danger to her person, to leave the residence of you, her husband, and she therefor [*sic*] prays that she may be deemed to have been deserted by you without

reasonable cause. That she is now at Manly aforesaid without means of support. That you are well able to support her but neglect to do.

These are therefore to command you, in His Majesty's name, to be and appear, on Wednesday the TENTH day of December 1902 at Ten O'clock in the forenoon at the Water Police Office, Sydney, in the said state, before such stipendiary Magistrate or Stipendary Magistrates for the Metropolitan Police District in the said state as may then be there, to answer to the complaint and to be further dealt with according to law.

GIVEN under my HAND AND SEAL, this sixth day of December in the year of our Lord, one thousand, nine hundred and two at Sydney in the said state.[5]

The summons was written with strikethroughs. The author of the document must have been in a hurry, or irritated. How many of these did he see a week?

Henry was on the record now. He was on notice. Friends of the unhappy couple gathered in corners. The end was coming.

But on that day, 6 December, Henry was found at the bottom of a cliff.

Extract from 'Lawson's Fall', an unpublished, handwritten poem by Henry Lawson, which was discovered among his papers, and probably composed in December 1902:

Twas the white clouds flying over, or the crawling sea below –
On the torture of the present or the dreams of long ago

Or the horror of the future born of black days fate – or all –
Never mind! The Gods who saw it know the cause of Lawson's fall.[6]

Where the Manly shore curves towards North Head, my friend Anna and I stop to swim in a tranquil sea. Afterwards the scrub- and rock-lined boardwalk warms our feet to Shelly Beach, where tents and towels are strewn across the sand.

At the back of the beach, we climb a track that leads up to the headland car park. The ocean sweeps to the horizon. Two wetsuited fishermen have climbed up some cliff steps. One of them is carrying a half-beheaded fish gutted through with a spear.

A council worker, in a high-vis jacket, slows his car. He leans forward.

'We're looking for Blue Fish Point,' I say.

'Dangerous there,' he warns.

He points out another track at the end of the car park. Trees tangle into scrub. We walk up rough rock steps covered in sandy dirt, into the bush.

'How dense would it have been when Henry walked – stumbled? – up here?' I think aloud. 'If there was this rocky track at all.'

A large white-and-red sign, graffitied with love initials, declares: 'DANGER warning! Achtung! Attenzione! Please be careful. Unfenced cliff and rocks. Ledges. Unstable surfaces.' Just in case you still don't understand, a stick figure stumbles over a cliff of tumbling rocks. Draw a moustache there, and this could be Henry. It's perilous up here, as much as in the rogue waves below.

The main path breaks open at the lookout. Here it's securely fenced over the drop to the fishermen on the rocks below. The scrub falls away with the sheer cliff face.

Anna turns to a couple beside us. 'Henry Lawson fell off this cliff,' she declares.

'Here? And he survived?' They are incredulous.

'It can't be here,' I say, perplexed. 'He would have died.'

'Did he fall? Or jump? Or was he drunk?' the guy asks. He's intrigued too.

'Probably all three,' I say. I'm looking for other paths.

'Who found him?' Anna asks, awed by the drop.

'A fisherman.'

According to a news article, the fisherman, Sly, was walking along the cliffs at 10 am when he saw a figure spreadeagled at the bottom of the cliff. Using a path fishermen used to get down to the rocks, he found that the man was Henry Lawson. It's unclear how long Henry was lying there before he was found.

Back along the main path, there's a side track with another danger sign. A large spider's web crosses among the trees. Beetles and baby spiders are caught in the web. We clamber over the sandstone, careful not to slip into the scrub.

This track also opens to an unfenced cliff top, jutting over the same point. We sit, our feet dangling over the edge. The fall undulates and jags, unlike the sheer drop at the lookout.

'This is more likely,' I venture. 'You could survive this. Especially if you were drunk.'

We silently contemplate it: a starry sunrise, a drunken poet, a cry in the dawn.

To Henry, residing in Sydney Hospital, dated 14 December 1902:

Dear Harry,

I'll come on Wednesday, with the children to see you (if possible). Any way eat all you can, and you will soon be well. I gave mother a shilling for stamps for you, and she said she'd take paper & etc. to you today …

I enclose a statement of accounts; so as you will see how I stand and how I spent the money. You see, I have to let the cottage or the rooms, then I will also go out and work because the rent and the furniture amount to 17/6 a week before a scrap of food is bought. I have answered advertisements both for work and boarders, and apartments and hav'n't had a single reply. If all else should fail, I can still go out and work by the day. I answered an advertisement for an assistant in a draper shop, but they didn't want me. I've heard nothing from the Bulletin re my story, so they apparently wish to treat me with silent contempt. If all else should fail I'll ask Bland Holt to give me a chance on the stage. I'll not go on the street. And I'd rather do that, than accept money from the Illingworth crowd.

Love from the kiddies & your wife
Bertha[7]

Bertha's 'statement of accounts' attached to her letter is an itemised list of everyday life: the chemist, one guinea; the rent, one pound; women minding the children, 12 shillings; cab and tram fares, laundry, lunch, butcher, baker, chicken and eggs. But she'd also included the cost of her lawyer – one guinea – and a 'Mr Blunden' – two guineas – and the 'Summons'es' – 8/10.

Imagine Henry's eye falling down the list, which then flutters onto the hospital bed. He is in pain, and the hospital can't fix it all.

The following month Henry wrote to *The Bulletin* about his fall at Manly:

Dear Bulletin,

Had a fall a week or two back – it wasn't the first. Some say eighty feet, some ninety and one man swore it was one hundred. I'll settle that with a tape-measure and the help of the man who picked me up – and another to hang on to my coat-tail – when I get on my feet again. Fell sheer, as far as I remember, and the condition of my clothes bears this out – coat and waist-coat all right; pants torn a little at knee and foot of one leg, one boot 'bust'. Landed between jagged rocks on bed of sand – or sand and rubble. Broke ankle and lost an eyebrow. (Pipe, tobacco and matches safe.)... Had whisky on board ... Heard or read somewhere that the first instinct of hurt animals is to crawl away and hide themselves. I distinctly remember, when I found myself alive, trying to crawl in under a shelf of rock with a wild idea of hiding. Attempt frustrated by one Sly, a fisherman, the burthen of whose song, to the top of the cliff, was, 'You're a lucky man! By ——, you *are* a lucky man! ...

When I was leaving the Casualty Ward of Sydney Hospital – which Chamber of Horrors I shall always remember kindly – I shook hands with a boy who'd had some toes cut off – a manly little fellow – and he said: 'Good-bye, Mr Lawson, better luck next time!' It sounded very funny to me.[8]

Henry, like most writers, couldn't resist turning a survival into a story. It's hard to believe that Henry didn't break his neck: all that was broken was an ankle. He was laid up in Sydney Hospital in the city, a celebrity patient. Mrs Byers, their former landlady in North Sydney, heard about Henry's accident from the papers. She and her niece bustled in to see him in the city:

> The next time we saw him was after he went over the cliffs at Manly Beach. I saw him in the hospital and what a wreck he looked. He was thin as a skeleton but how pleased he was to see us. A niece of mine was with me and he held onto us as if he feared we would leave him too soon ... We went to see him again, but he had gone out though still on crutches. We called to see his mother in Phillip St. She spoke kindly of him but said that Harry should never have left her, and that his proper place was with her.[9]

Mrs Byers confided that a revolver was taken from Henry by the doctor, and then returned with great reluctance after he requested it. The doctor told Mrs Byers: 'Seeing that this is Mr Lawson's property, I have no right to it, but tell Mr Lawson to be careful how he uses it.' Mrs Byers remembered: 'As soon as Lawson received it again he sold it.'[10]

Bertha hurried and flurried to his bedside. She wrote in between visits to Sydney Hospital, and then again when he had moved to another 'rest hospital' – for his depression and alcoholism rather than his continued recovery from his injuries. When he was released home, she was by his side, watching in case he should fall once more, and not just over a cliff.

A gossip item appeared in *The Critic*, on 28 February 1903, about

Lawson looking well and strong:

> Henry Lawson has now quite recovered from the effects of his
> fall over the Manly Cliffs, but is usually accompanied on his
> walks abroad by Mrs. Lawson – in case he should slip again, as
> it were. He is brighter and cheerier than he has been for years.
> His accident threw him out of the running for the time, but
> he has a continual commission from English magazines, and
> some Australian papers. It is scarcely likely that the Lawsons will
> return to England. Henry would like to go, he can hear better
> amid the din of London than elsewhere, but Mrs. Lawson says
> that she would want £1,000 a week to live in Bourke (N.S.W.)
> and would sooner live in Bourke than in London.[11]

His near-death experience had reunited them for a few more
months, and the desertion charge that Bertha had lodged in Manly
Court in December seemed, if not forgotten, at least in abeyance.
One last chance. *Dearie, let's forget the past.*

I remember a family trip to Whale Beach, during a tense time in our
marriage. It was the beach where Dan had once drawn 'I love you'
on my back soon after we'd met. On this trip, my young niece and
I went for a swim while Dan stayed on the beach with his father.
The water was rough, and deceptively shallow. My niece swam into
a swirl of sand and struggled. I swam in after her.

'It's okay,' I said as she panicked. 'Hold on. Try to float.'

I didn't want to let her go, in case she disappeared. We were so
close to the shore, but the current was pulling us away. We trod
water as the waves washed back and forth around us.

I saw Dan in the distance. He was looking at us.

'Dan!' I cried, swallowing water. I waved – not the calm signal for help you are supposed to make, but a drowning plea. He grabbed a boogie board and swam out. We clutched on to its foam as it rocked in the water with our weight.

'It's a rip,' he said.

I nodded, afraid to talk again in case I swallowed more water. A surfer paddled over and, looking up, I saw a helicopter hovering above, supervising the rescue as the surfer and Dan helped us kick out of the rip to a sandbank. We hugged and kissed on the beach as my niece flopped on the sand, exhausted, with a towel around her shaking body.

'Thank you,' I said, kissing him again.

Thinking back, that rescue probably gave our marriage another good six months.

10

From Ladywood, Whistler St, Manly, Wednesday, undated but thought to be in 1903:

My Dear Harry,

I am writing as promised. Why did you ask me to go to day. You can never know what an awful struggle I had with myself to come & see you. You know dear, if you would rather we were parted, *I am willing*. And it would be best to part now, we have made the break, and you did not seem a bit pleased to see me. Would you rather we separated?

I must know this. I have suffered. God alone knows. You never understood me and never will. Now through your family, I have to fight for my reputation. I have scarcely a friend, even Dr Bennett turned from me, it is always the case. A man gets every one's sympathy. (I can live it all down) Dr Bennett need not have said what he did. Of course when you are drunk, you are not responsible for what you say. But your cursed relatives go and verify your drunken statements. If you wish us to come together again it is on the understanding not a relative of yours darkens our door. I will never speak to Peter or your Mother so long as I live. She can go where people can see her and shed her crocodile tears and make a blessed fuss, but she would not put her hand in her pocket and give your children a sixpence. I hate her. Now Harry I want to impress on your mind. I'll have no deceit. It must be all or nothing with me. I have forgiven you. And I never thought I could do it. You asked me to go to day (after all I had done). Never mind I'm glad you told me. It is better to say what we think. Still I feel now when you care to see me you will send for me. I would not come unless, don't think I will come, if you do not wish to see me. Mind Harry, I am quite agreeable to the Separation. I came to you and you asked me to go. Now you must send for me. I felt it because I suffered so terribly, in forgiving.

Still all that is over. I have stopped all law proceedings, and I hope you will soon be well and strong again. You have plenty of sympathizers, plenty who will shield you, behind the slanders of your wife. I think I have the courage to live it all down. If I wanted to love another man, or go wrong, it was not for lack of opportunity. You know my ideas of life, and you also know you are the only man I ever cared for. It is cruel the report should be round I forced you in to a marriage. Any way. My own heart & conscience is the only comfort I have.

Love from your children & your wife,
Bertha[1]

Louisa, Henry's mother, looms over the narrative. She was an unofficially separated woman herself, having left her husband, Peter, in the bush to move to Sydney in 1883. She was formidable. The severity of the 19th-century photographs accentuates her strength. Henry called her 'The Chieftain'. She was such a memorable woman that she has transcended the status of 'Poet's Mother' to being memorable in her own right.

Louisa was only 18 when she married Peter; the author of *Louisa*, Brian Matthews, writes that Louisa at this age was 'a magnificent looking young woman, volatile, passionate, even in a way mysterious'.[2]

Similarities between Henry and his father affected both their wives. Like Henry, who was a 'confirmed drinker' when he and Bertha married, Peter, 34, was a confirmed gold miner when he and Louisa married in similar haste in 1866. Matthews observes, 'To the day he died and despite the constant necessity to attend full time to other tasks, Peter continued to think about gold, theorise about it, and above all, seek it.'[3] Henry's relationship with alcohol seems the same. He thought about it; he wrote about it; and, above all, he sought it out.

Peter and his bride also moved to the goldfields, where according to *Louisa*, Henry was famously born at Grenfell 'in a tent by a flooded gully' the following year.[4] His younger sister, Gertrude, later wrote what she'd been told of his dramatic birth: 'Flood waters isolated the little camp when Henry chose to enter the world and the nurse had to be carried over miles of yellow waters.'[5] Colin Roderick, however, pours cold water on this memory. He attests that Henry was born in a hut, not a tent, and there was no tempest[6] – although Louisa, in the throes of 19th-century childbirth, would surely not have known or cared much about the weather.

Their brother, Charles, followed; then another brother, Peter; and finally the twins. But while baby Gertrude survived, her sister Annette perished soon after birth.

The grieving mother felt her intellect perishing too. After five more years, Louisa left the drought-stricken farm and her absent husband on the goldfields, only taking with her to Sydney Gertrude, five, and her third youngest, Peter, nine. I recognise it as one of those moments in which you know you are defining yourself.

How did 16-year-old Henry feel when he was left behind? With his father so often away, he'd been by his mother's side, taking his father's place on the farm. But this time Louisa left when Henry was away at the diggings too, helping his father, so he received the news that his mother had gone to Sydney while reading her letter with his dad.

Yet the similarities between them remained in the shadows. Mary Gilmore wrote that, soon after she met Henry, Louisa had sent him to collect maintenance owed by his father, which had abruptly stopped. 'I recalled that Mrs Lawson was very bitter about it and threatened law action. Henry went on my advice and came back his father's friend.' Mary said that Henry had discovered his father had been ill and 'for a week had lain in his hut with no food'.[7]

Brian Matthews notes that, at the time Louisa left the family farm, younger brother Charlie had not been heard of for months. He'd disappeared after being flogged and mock-hanged by his father. Many perennially absent parents double the discipline when they are at home, as if to double their presence. Matthews writes of the day the boy left home:

> The silent and dangerous diggings ring with Louisa's strong voice
> calling 'Charlieee, Charlieee ...' But he is not at the bottom of

an abandoned shaft; he is heading for Granville, two hundred miles away ... For Charlie it is the beginning of nearly twenty years of wandering and petty crime.[8]

Henry is not the only tragedy in the family. He is just the one everyone remembers.

Louisa was a spiritualist as well as a pragmatist; after she died, Henry would recall her holding a séance during his youth, in his sketch 'Table Legs, Wooden Heads and a Woman's Heart'.[9] In Sydney, Louisa embraced the political spirit of the suffragettes. She launched Australia's first women's magazine, *The Dawn*, using women printers only, and then challenged men-only unionisation when her printing was stopped because of her employment policy.

When Henry followed his mother to Sydney, he earned money painting trains, and then became inspired by faces in the street. Mother and son collaborated on his first book. They clashed over his romance with Bertha; and then clashed again when Louisa published an anthology of his work without permission, while he and Bertha were living in New Zealand. She sounds both fascinating and frightening. The ultimate mother-in-law.

Although Louisa always focused on her latest crusade, rather than on Henry and Bertha, was blood thicker than feminism when their marriage unravelled?

Reading between the lines, dislike of Louisa radiates from the yellowed text in Bertha's memoir:

Harry's sensitiveness and sympathy ... in my opinion he inherited them from his father's Norse blood ...

Louisa was a remarkable character, a very determined woman and she and her poet son could never see eye to eye. Apart they remained friendly; together they soon were at daggers-drawn …

Harry's mother lived with us for a time at Manly, when Jim was a small boy. Apart from that time, we rarely saw her during our life together, except in times of sickness, when she sent for us.[10]

She could 'shed her crocodile tears', wrote Bertha, the drunkard's wife. 'I hate her.'

But a quieter family voice comes from Henry's younger sister, Gertrude, in her own memories, also lodged at the Mitchell Library. The sheaves of paper from the family, from Mary, from Mrs Byers, all bristle with opinions about Henry and Bertha. Torn between loyalty to her brother and a woman's view of Bertha's situation, Gertrude weighed in: 'The blame rested on Harry. His inebriation was a factor. Some of the responsibility lay with her highly-strung temperament. They were better off apart.'[11]

Diana, the mother of Dan and Mariana, died before I met Dan, so I never had to negotiate a relationship with her through the marriage. Ruby was given Diana as her second name, as a tribute to the woman neither she nor I ever knew. I once asked Mariana what her mother was like.

'You are like her,' Mariana said. 'Imagine you with conspiracy theories.'

'Me?' I questioned. 'Really? I thought she was an opera singer.'

'She was, but she was a journalist and producer for the ABC,' Mariana said. 'She wrote novels. She was a Leo too. I think Dan married his mother.'

Families split and then entwine in different ways. These days Mariana and I still share everything with each other, rolling our eyes over a man who is her brother, her niece's father and my ex-husband.

'You know him,' she told me recently. 'You don't have any expectations. You understand the person he is.'

Waiting for Dan at the airport on one of his infrequent visits home, Ruby was draped over the rail in the arrivals hall while I hung back with Mariana and their older sister, who had accompanied us. We were like the three witches in *Macbeth*, conjuring up reasons to keep him in the country so he could spend more time with his daughter.

'A woman,' his older sister decided. 'Let's set him up with someone.'

The thought was lost as he appeared in the crowd.

11

Handwritten letter in purple pencil, Sunday, undated:

Dear Bertha

Was sorry I spoke harshly to you on Saturday, knowing the
state of your nerves: but you knew the state of my health and
should not have told me about that vile slander nor hinted that
you believed it.

Will send money in a day or two.

Harry

<u>If you want me home send write at once.</u> Yes or No

Come to me on Monday (today).[1]

On a damp winter's day, in the warm reading room of the State Library Victoria, I sit down to Bertha's original letters, contained in a plastic sleeve in an archival box. They are decaying and lined with time.

When the sea breezes had turned autumn cool, tension tugged at the marriage again. The loops in Bertha's words curled with distress, with caring questions, despair, anxiety, then curt demands.

Bertha was beyond the reason why. She was angry and hurt that his family and his friends were verifying his 'drunken statements'.

I have the courage to live it all down.

She wrote again in March or April 1903:

'Ladywood',
Whistler St.
Manly.
Monday

Darling

just a line, Dr Hall has just called in to ask after you, he told me to tell you he'll be up to see you the first day he can get away. Harry he is your truest and staunchest friend, don't you let your delusions carry you away in this matter, believe me in this matter. I'm a woman and I know men, think of all he did for you. And he has shielded you, all though [*sic*] Manly. And he will take a great interest in you still. You be your true self to him, tell him you never meant what you said when you were drunk – you know you were so cruel to him that morning, when he came to get you into Prince Alfred Hospital. Tell him also I'm not the black woman I'm painted. I would feel it if he believed me bad because he is one of the few men I have any respect for. I respect about five men in the world, and I hope they also respect me. I love one – does he love me.

I will bring the children to see you on Wednesday. Dearie I owe Dr Hall my reason and my life. If it had not been for him, I should certainly have gone mad, and I'd have taken my own life to. So that is why I want you to be nice to him and thank him for all he has done.

Why don't you write to me I'm so lonely. I get very miserable at times. Do you think of me. Ah, dearie, do let us forget the past. And we'll try and make the future bright for each other, hurry up and get well. And we will commence a new life here by the sea. We won't have any relatives, and only those who have proved themselves friends. Do you ever think of me I often do of you, and wonder if you are thinking of me – think and sum me all up from the first you have known of me. Now don't you think I've tried hard to forgive you, haven't I done all in my power. Harry, do you love me as much as I love you.

Love from your children and your lonely wife
Bertha.

Don't be influenced by anything your Mother or brother says.[2]

Henry was becoming blunt in response to her long pleas. On the Sunday, there was no poetry or romantic letter. He had reached for the nearest pencil, a purple one, and scrawled the question: *If you want me home … yes or no?*

105

Henry moved in again with Mrs Byers at the Coffee Palace in North Sydney. Mrs Byers, Henry's 'little woman', was sturdy and Scottish.

> It made my heart ache to see him in such grief. He sat down with his arms on one of the tables and cried. My place was full, but I turned one of the pretty tearooms into a room. He was happy, and it made me happy too.[3]

Her home was demolished long ago, and a modernist, 14-storey building spreads down the block instead. Looking at the new tower, I think the best marriages are like heritage buildings. They withstand stress and change. They weather regret, conflict and failings. They seem to overcome the restless search for the new. They are worn with time, yet restored because of their faith in their foundations.

Bertha's lonely letter showed her foundation was shaken.

Harry, do you love me as much as I love you?

Dearie, my heart is breaking.[4]

Letter to George Robertson, dated 26 April 1903 from the Prince Alfred Hospital, Sydney:

Dear R.,

I am here remanded for medical treatment – drunk. She (Mrs L.) has taken out a legal separation, but will forgive me.

[H.L.][5]

Henry's publisher, George Robertson, remained a diplomat between Mr and Mrs Lawson. Bertram Stevens initially tried to help too. He recalled:

> They asked me to fix up the matter privately, & agreed to the form I prepared. Lawson however, came to me afterwards & wanted me to bluff his wife & prevent her from completing the separation. I advised Mrs Lawson to go to a solicitor & apply for the judicial separation, which she did. It was clear to me at the time that Lawson was very fond of his wife & loath to lose her, yet it was impossible for them to be happy together.[6]

But Henry always wanted reconciliation, said Mrs Byers. This wasn't a mutual separation, which is the easiest, rather than the roulette of what-still-can-be. A clean split offers the relief of agreement. Irreconcilable differences.

Except Henry thought their differences were reconcilable. Imagine Henry cajoling like we might today: *Just another shot. Things will change. You'll see. C'mon. Let's try again. I love you.* Bertha seems to have wavered in March or April too. The reality of single parenting – all the space in her bed and none in her life – elicited, I knew, stark feelings.

There was a future still underlining Bertha's letters. She thought there was a chance too. It's exhausting – all this hope for reconciliation and change, then once more realising that things are the same. I recognise how she felt.

Mrs Byers recalled that Henry 'often hoped and wished that the estrangement would be bridged … his hopes on this matter were very high … He was hoping that some place could be taken in the country where he would be able to settle down with Mrs Lawson. He was very disappointed when the arrangements broke down.'[7]

My gypsy friend who lived on a yacht was all at sea after a sudden family breakup.

'I told the kids, "Your father has abandoned ship. He's left me to deal with the boat and all this shit." The boat's a tip and the kids won't help. They ask me for money and I tell them, "I don't have it." You know what? He can have the kids too and see how he likes it.'

Then, six months after the split, she's sent the kids down south to live with their dad, who wants them to live with him too. The boat's being sold.

'I've got to get my career back. I've spent the last 15 years working towards living on this boat. For what?' She's studying to be a captain and plans to work on other people's boats for a while. 'Maybe I'll work on boats overseas. All I can think about is Thailand. I'm so tired after this shit.'

'I had that feeling,' I say. 'I fantasised about falling asleep under a palm tree for a week.'

She flails. 'The kids say all I do is yell, and I tell them, "Well, that's because you don't do anything I ask you to." Anyway. The kids are better off with him. I'm too toxic right now.'

'No, you're not,' I correct. 'You've been a single parent and doing everything. It pulls you down sometimes.'

Soon after our conversation, she posts a picture on Facebook of a forlorn cardboard man next to a sign that reads: 'If you want to know who your true friends are, lose everything you own and see who is still standing by your side.'

Poem by Henry Lawson, published in 1905 in *When I Was King and Other Verses*:

The Separation

We knew too little of the world,
    And you and I were good –
'Twas paltry things that wrecked our lives
    As well I knew they would.
The people said our love was dead,
    But how were they to know?
Ah! had we loved each other less
    We'd not have quarrelled so.

We knew too little of the world,
    And you and I were kind,
We listened to what others said
    And both of us were blind.

The people said 'twas selfishness,
    But how were they to know?
Ah! had we both more selfish been
    We'd not have parted so.

But still when all seems lost on earth
    Then heaven sets a sign –
Kneel down beside your lonely bed,
    And I will kneel by mine,
And let us pray for happy days –
    Like those of long ago.
Ah! had we knelt together then
    We'd not have parted so.[1]

In the State Library Victoria, scrolls of old poem proofs are as ragged and marked as Henry became. He mourned the separation and feared his children not knowing him in the drift of fatherhood after divorce. He sent the poem 'The Separation' to Bertha.[2]

We separate to protect ourselves. But the most telling of all detachments is how we depersonalise those with whom we've lost the most intimate of connections. A male friend refers to his ex as 'the mother'. Or worse: 'It's the thing that gave birth to my child,' a man spits at a barbecue when reading a phone text from his child's mother.

Henry and Bertha depersonalised their relationship too. Love letters, poems and endearments made way for formal correspondence communicated via lawyers. 'Darling' and 'Girlie' became 'Mrs Lawson'.

Mrs Byers saw this flatlining too, as her biographer recounted:

Lawson often acted impulsively. One day he saw Mrs Lawson with her child in North Sydney. He went up straight away and kissed the child, but took no notice of Mrs Lawson. Naturally Mrs Lawson was very indignant, and the same evening, called at Mrs Byers' house. Mrs Lawson told her that if she did not keep Henry away from her, she would shoot him.[3]

I have lunch with my former assistant editor, Tracy, with whom I was working in the lead-up to, and through, my divorce.

We swap stories about colleagues scattered between the UK and Australia. Some, like Tracy, have become mothers too and are seeking the elusive work–life balance that is always talked about, but in reality rarely happens.

'What do you remember of that time when I split up with Dan?' I ask her. I'm always seeking other perspectives. 'I don't know how I did it.'

'I must say I don't know how you did it either,' she replies. 'You did seem a bit of a shambles back then ... you seemed very vulnerable and overwhelmed. You just sort of got on with things, but you did look pretty stressed and unhappy. I remember passing you one day on the bus on the way to work – it was pouring with rain and you didn't have an umbrella. You were getting soaked and I remember thinking that you were probably so preoccupied with getting Ruby out the door that it didn't even occur to you to keep yourself dry.'

'That happened the other day, I was caught in a sudden thunderstorm without an umbrella. So I think that's me ...'

'I remember you telling me how stressful it was getting her to school and then to work on time,' Tracy continues. 'Ruby would refuse to put her shoes on and then you'd miss the bus. Now that I'm a mother, I marvel all the more at how you not only managed to get through that, but you were writing a book in the middle of it all. I remember at the time that I – and many of your friends – felt you were letting Dan off quite lightly and we felt that when you left him it was long overdue.'

Two women hold on to the edge of the pool and kick in tandem, their hair pushed under caps. They chat as they splash: 'So I texted him. I was polite. I said, "It's clear we have different interests. Let's leave it before this goes on for long." He texted back – get this! – "Yeah, I think so too. Your political tone annoyed me." My tone! My tone!' Their kicking stops and they stand up. 'I wanted to text back. Then I thought – leave it.'

If only ending a marriage was that simple. A text. *Let's leave it. Take care.* Instead, there are reams of formalities, even when the two parties are amicable. Dan and I needed a Justice of the Peace to sign off a mutual consent form, then a court date to formally end it, because we had a child. The alternative was for one of us to serve papers on the other, which seemed unnecessary and fractious.

During one of his brief visits home the year after we separated, I filled out my bit of the papers and took them to the beach house where he and Ruby were staying.

'We need to do this today,' I said to him, as he cut up his breakfast mango.

'Are you getting married again?' he asked.

'No,' I said. 'I want to know that it's done.'

I crashed that night on the sofa, and early the next morning I swam in the ocean pool. As I stroked I felt a weight slide off one of my fingers. I duck-dived down to the sand, searching for a glint of gold. For the first time in my married life, my wedding ring had slipped off my finger.

In tears, I kept looking. The water was still that day, so the sand was stable.

'Is this it?' a swimmer called, holding up the rose-gold ring.

'Yes, thank you,' I said, and slipped it back onto my right hand, where it had lived since we separated. I jokingly called it my divorce finger. Today that was going to actually be true.

I hurried back to the house. 'So we are doing this today,' I said.

Dan was sleepy. 'Yeah.'

'Yeah,' I said, determined. The loss of the ring seemed too significant to ignore.

All thoughts of dignified ceremonies having been put aside, I searched online for a local JP. The nearby chemist was one. Right.

Dan dressed and insisted on doing some piano practice first. Lunch first. Anything first.

'Dan. Please.'

He looked upset. 'I don't know why this is so important to you,' he said. 'Let's just wait until one of us needs to do it.'

'It's our marriage. And who knows when you'll be back in the country. What if you meet someone?'

We walked in silence to the chemist. At the rear counter, among prescriptions and hair products and barefoot children begging their parents for an ice cream, we asked for the chemist.

He looked between us. People queued behind us, interested.

We signed the papers. He signed too.

'Thanks, mate,' Dan said.

I took the papers, slipping them back into the plastic sleeve, and we walked out of the chemist, and our marriage.

113

The earliest divorce files are held at the State Records Authority of NSW in Kingswood. The cab travels along roads lined with gum trees to this archive in the bush.

'What's out here?' the cabbie asks.

'State records,' I reply. 'Historical documents.'

He's a chatty driver. 'What are you researching?'

'Divorce,' I answer. 'I'm trying to find out about a divorce a century ago.'

'Is it hard to get a divorce?' he asks.

'Then? Yes. It was really hard. I didn't realise you could even do it until I started researching this project.'

'What about now?' he asks. 'I mean, what do you have to do?'

I think back to my own divorce. My lawyer had wanted me to state when and where her father could see Ruby.

'When he is in the country will be great,' I'd replied.

'Are you sure?' she'd asked. 'Don't you want to specify when he can see your daughter?' She was taken aback. She was used to formalising hand-over times, and who had the children on birthdays and Christmas. It was too loose, she argued.

'I can't pin him to dates and times,' I explained. 'I have no idea.'

On the steps of the Family Court, after a hearing that only lasted a few minutes, she'd said, 'Easiest divorce I've ever done.'

Yet I know of divorces that drag on for years in a vicious wrangle for custody and assets. One man became so close to his lawyers that they came to his Christmas party.

'It depends,' I finally tell the cab driver.

In the State Records building hidden among half-cleared scrub, the old divorce files are rolled in ribbon and labelled in calligraphy.

There's a ceremonial respect here for the end of an undertaking that was supposed to last until death. The divorce certificate of today is in plain black type – an expression of how routine it is now to produce the piece of paper that will allow us to begin again.

By 1879, the *Evening News* declared: 'The records of the Divorce Court in this colony show that the number of suits has been quite as prolific as at first anticipated.'[4] The article reported that 106 cases had been heard since the *Matrimonial Causes Act* had been introduced in 1873; 50 of those marriages were dissolved; and 20 decrees nisi granted, awaiting further proceedings to make them absolute. The rest, the paper reported, had either been abandoned or were awaiting trial. The third-ever petition was by Mary Kirkham Wilson, who dared to divorce her husband on one of the three grounds permitted: desertion for more than three years.[5] Conditional adultery and cruelty, also for three years and upwards, were the two other grounds available.

That so few people, and so rarely women, dared to divorce reveals the difficulty and distress of such a drastic action. There were not only the daunting legalities but also the gossip and public reporting, which from the start turned the Divorce Court proceedings into 'a spectator sport'.

Imagine Mary entering the courthouse, nervously crossing the black-and-white marble floor of the foyer, and waiting under the soaring dome ceiling. The air was musty from the Tank Stream running below, which caused perpetual seepage. The courthouse was already bulging with criminals, and now with divorcing husbands and wives.

In neat black ink on blue-lined paper, Mary wrote that her husband Robert and the 'adulteress Isabella had boarded the *Atrevida* to San Francisco'. It was such a serious business, this first woman wanting a divorce, that the Divorce Court summoned the Master of the *Atrevida* to confirm her story.

'They called themselves Mr and Mrs Smith,' the Master recalled. 'Then later he said his name was actually Robert Wilson. They shared a master cabin.'

The court tried to summon Robert Wilson, aka Mr Smith, back to Sydney from San Francisco. Unsurprisingly, he didn't respond and he was divorced in absentia.

Rolling up Mary's file with its elegant white ribbon, proud of her for what she did, I unfurl the Lawson case, No. 4676.

Bertha's first police action alleging desertion and cruelty in December 1902 had resulted in an interim order for 'maintenance and support for the said defendant's deserted wife' from January 1903.[6] Recognition of desertion was an early version of child support and did not necessarily require judicial separation – which Bertha then pursued in April 1903 – or the full-decree absolute divorce. It seems quite amazing, when I think about it, that there was provision for deserted wives at all; but I'm being blinded by an assumption that, prior to the 1970s, little if any consideration was given to those who had to forge lives apart.

However, the law of desertion only covered married mothers. Single mothers outside wedlock were seen as makers of their own folly, and subjected to unmarried mothers' homes, forced adoptions and stigmatised poverty. Bertha told Henry that she had 'to fight for her reputation'; but with the ring on her hand – well, until she pawned it – she had a reputation to fight for.

But this was only 1903 and the acknowledgment of no fault was still over 70 years away. The initial NSW *Matrimonial Causes Act*

1873 allowed either the husband or the wife to petition the court to enforce a return to conjugal rights.

Predictably, the law was biased. If a wife committed adultery, this was sufficient to allow any husband to obtain a divorce 'on the ground that his wife has since the celebration thereof been guilty of adultery'.[7]

The Act then stated the grounds on which a wife could petition for divorce in cases of adultery. The circumstances were extreme, as if the exhaustion of a marriage breakdown and rumours of real affairs weren't enough:

> And it shall be lawful for any wife to present a petition to the Court praying that her marriage may be dissolved on the ground that since the celebration thereof her husband has been guilty of incestuous adultery, or of bigamy with adultery or of rape or of sodomy or of bestiality or of adultery coupled with such cruelty as without adultery would have entitled her to a divorce *a mensa et thoro* under the law heretofore existing in England or of adultery coupled with desertion without reasonable excuse for two years and upwards.[8]

By 1903, the Act had been amended, for those wives who could prove they lived in New South Wales, to allow divorces for adultery pure and simple. In addition, a divorcing wife could claim if she could prove her husband's continual desertion, his drunkenness leading to her being left 'without the means of support', or his habitual cruelty, for three years or upwards; his imprisonment for at least three years, being sentenced to death, or frequent convictions in five years; a recent conviction for his attempt to murder her or intent to cause her grievous bodily harm; or her being repeatedly assaulted and cruelly beaten for one year. The conditions for the lesser judicial separation, as Bertha eventually chose, were simpler: desertion without cause for at least two years, or, adultery or cruelty for two years and upwards.[9]

Hannah Thornburn was a ghost now; if Bertha wanted to invoke the adultery clause, she could not subpoena a spirit. Hear the breathlessness in her voice, the rising stress, the anxiety to convince. *And, and, and. Then, then, then.* Words start off as a soft, secure verbal embrace. But then, as love turns, words slap and spit.

The court records it all.

13

To Henry Lawson from his solicitor, dated 4 June 1903:

Dear Sir,

Your and Mrs Lawson's decree for judicial separation without admissions was made this morning by consent on terms filed in court. No evidence was heard and no pleadings read the whole affair occupying one minute.

I interviewed the reporters and also Mr Saunders of the Star. At any rate there is very little to publish.

I received on your behalf £2 for Mrs Lawson on Tuesday and paid same to Mr Henderson.

Yours truly,
James Elphinstone[1]

Despite all the hurdles and the laborious necessity of proof, in the 30 years from 1873 to *Lawson v. Lawson* in 1903, the number of divorce applications leapt to 400 couples a year.[2] The amended *Matrimonial Causes Act 1899* had already wised up to the hiding and selling of assets to avoid alimony; it stated in section 59:

(1) Where it appears to the Court that a sale of real estate is about to be made with intent to defeat a petitioner's claim in respect of costs alimony or the maintenance of the children or damages on the ground of adultery the Court may by order restrain the sale or order the proceeds of the sale to be paid into the Court to be dealt with as the Court directs.[3]

Though it is unlikely Bertha would have thanked her mother-in-law for anything, Louisa's magazine had supported those suffragettes who first lobbied for the deserted mothers, left in the dust of the gold rush, and then later for the wives deserted for drink. Louisa had her own experience as a gold miner's wife, although Peter had promised financial support in Sydney. Introducing *The Dawn* in 1888, Louisa reflected, 'Men legislate on divorce, on hours of labor, and many another question intimately affecting women, but neither ask nor know the wishes of those whose lives and happiness are most concerned.'[4]

The pioneering women had worked with parliamentary reformer Attorney-General WC Windeyer to obtain the *Divorce Amendment and Extension Act of 1892* in the colony of New South Wales, mirroring a similar law enacted two years previously in Victoria. Supporting the 1890 Victorian divorce law in *The Dawn* with an editorial titled 'The Divorce Extension Bill or The Drunkard's Wife', Louisa wrote, 'The fate of the Victorian divorce extension bill is a source of keen anxiety to many a miserable wife who has the misfortune to be linked for life to a drunkard.'[5]

Her article, published prior to Henry's marriage to Bertha, was prescient of her future daughter-in-law's predicament:

All the consolation the wife of such a ghoul could reasonably expect from the world is 'Why did you marry him?' About as reasonable a question as asking a condemned criminal awaiting his execution why he committed the act that brought him there. What availeth her to say 'I was young, ignorant, inexperienced in the ways of the world, I believed and I loved him: he vowed that I should not want; he loved me and would love me forever; all these promises he has broken. I have kept mine. He will not support me; he drinks and is cruel to me.' And the world's answer is: 'As you have made your bed so you must lie on it.' A wife's heart must be the tomb of her husband's faults.[6]

Henry, I kept my promise.

After Bertha's affidavit to the Divorce Court, Henry was served with notice by the Registrar:

Whereas Bertha Marie Louise Lawson claiming to have been lawfully married to you the withinnamed Respondent has filed her Petition in the Matrimonial Causes Jurisdiction of our said Court praying that she may be judicially separated from you wherein the said Bertha Marie Louisa [*sic*] Lawson alleges that you have been guilty of habitual drunkenness and cruelty for three years immediately preceding the date of the filing of the said Petition. Now This Is To Command You that within fourteen days after service hereof ... you cause an appearance to be entered for you in our said Court to the said Petition AND TAKE NOTICE that in default of your so doing our said Court will proceed to hear the said charges proved in due course of law ...[7]

A month after Bertha lodged the judicial separation, *The Critic*, barely bothering to conceal Henry's identity, had revealed in the 'personal gossip' section of 30 May:

A certain Australian writer has been lately gravitating from the lock-up to the hospital with surprising swiftness. His wife has left him and attends to apply for a judicial separation. Some folks have been writing sympathetically about the strain of overwork that drives so many Australasian literary men astray. It is not overwork, but over drink which is to blame as a rule. The trouble is, to paraphrase Kendall:– The lot of beer that waits upon the man of letters here.[8]

14

In the Supreme Court of New South Wales, Matrimonial Causes Jurisdiction No. 4676 between Bertha Marie Louise Lawson, petitioner, and Henry Lawson, respondent, Thursday, the fourth day of June in the year of our Lord, one thousand, nine hundred and three. Written in ink calligraphy.

Upon reading the petition filed herein on the sixth day of April last past and upon reading the notice of motion filed herein on the twenty eighth day of May last past and upon hearing Mr Robert Newburn Henderson attorney for the petitioner and Mr Hammond of counsel for the respondent who appeared to consent <u>this court doth by consent without admissions Order and Decree</u> that Bertha Marie Louise Lawson the petitioner herein be and she is hereby judicially separated from Henry Lawson the respondent and that the petitioner do have the sole custody of the children and that the respondent do have access to the children one afternoon in each week and <u>this court doth</u>

<u>further order</u> the respondent to pay alimony to the petitioner and maintenance for the children at the rate of thirty shillings per week for a period of three months from the date of decree herein with leave reserved to Bertha Marie Louise Lawson the said petitioner to apply subsequently for further alimony for herself and maintenance for said children and this court doth further order that the said respondent do pay to Messieurs Beeby and Henderson the solicitors for the petitioner the sum of twenty guineas the petitioner's costs herein within the following fines, namely: seven pounds during the month of June, instant, seven pounds during the month of July next and seven pounds during the month of August next.

For the Court
Arthur Gluddington [unconfirmed spelling]
Deputy Registrar[1]

On 4 June 1903, already weary of subpoenaing deserted husbands, seeking evidence from ship captains and receiving the assurances of adulteresses, Justice George Simpson, peering over a moustache that rivalled Henry's, only wanted the terms of settlement. That Henry would not admit to any allegations of habitual drunkenness or cruelty, that he wanted his marriage to continue, was now an irritation rather than an obstacle. Henry was in hospital at the time, denying the press their celebrity witness.

Unconstrained by the later *Family Law Act*, which upon its inception in 1975 prevented the publication of family law matters so as to 'enhance the dignity of the divorce process', *The Sydney Morning Herald* reported the Lawson hearing on 5 June 1903, along with two other cases heard in the Divorce Court. Florence Lamb had sought a divorce from her husband, Robert Kitson Lamb, absent in South Africa, but 'the case was adjourned till Thursday next for the production of further evidence'. In the other case, Emily Lennon had sought dissolution of her marriage on the grounds of desertion, but 'his Honor suggested that the petition should be amended … as the evidence in support of the ground of desertion was not sufficient, whereas there was evidence of the respondent's drunkenness and leaving the petitioner without support for three years and upwards'.[2]

The Sydney Morning Herald offered spectators the last word in the Lawson case: 'By consent a decree for judicial separation was granted in the case of Bertha Marie Louise Lawson, formerly Bredt, versus Henry Lawson, author and journalist.'[3]

In a letter, Bertha had written to Henry, 'I dread the publicity.' Perhaps to save Henry's reputation, and her privacy, the charges that Bertha laid out in her affidavit were not heard in court and the marriage was now reduced to a file number; 'the whole affair occupying one minute,' as James Elphinstone briskly told his client. The separation option allowed for couples to live legally apart, and for child and spousal support to be paid: it became a marriage in name only, literally. Filed at the State Records, the document is rolled up with Bertha's affidavit and tied with a pink ribbon – a present from the past, ceremoniously and carefully labelled in calligraphy, its beauty hiding the ugliness of the events that caused it.

On a Saturday morning at the top of the harbour cliff stairs from Woolloomooloo wharf to Potts Point, I encounter runners and dog walkers staring up at a scaffolded tower, slippery from overnight rain. A man in a white shirt and blue shorts, who looks like he should be sitting at a cafe table for brunch, is climbing up the steel.

'Brother, come down,' a voice in the crowd pleads.

'These people pay their mortgages by ripping apart my kids' lives,' he shouts back from his precarious perch.

Police sirens speed to the scene.

Since the introduction of the *Family Law Act 1975*, which emphasised no fault, it's never been easier to divorce. And yet people are still voluntarily filing their allegations and defences. To prove they are the better parent, the wronged wife, the harangued husband.

Order. Order!

Isn't that the demand for calm?

Since Bertha and Henry separated, more than a century has passed. What really has changed?

Henry, you are dead to me.

Awarded a judicial separation of *a mensa et thoro* – Latin for 'from table and bed' – Bertha was now formally separated from Henry. The updated *Matrimonial Causes Act 1899* preferred 'dissolution of marriage' to 'divorce'. She had her separation, and with that the assurance of child support and the ability to keep any assets that she acquired from that point on. There weren't any assets anyway. They'd lost their furniture because of unpaid rent.

How did she spend the rest of the day after the judicial separation was heard? Did she feel relieved? Sad? Numb? In her memoir she only recalled:

we remained in Manly living with a very kind woman, Mrs. Ellison, who took care of the children while I went to work. Harry often came to see us but it was useless taking up house again as he was quite penniless and the children had to be provided for. He undoubtedly had some resentment about this situation, but I told him he would always be welcome to come and see us. And so the years passed on.[4]

After my own court hearing, conducted while Ruby was at school, I was dazed. The event matched what Henry's lawyer had said, 'the whole affair only taking one minute'. Dan was away, somewhere.

Afterwards, before going back to work, I went to my lunchtime yoga. I must have looked distracted. I think I stopped mid-pose.

'Are you alright?' the yoga instructor asked.

'Yes. Just got divorced,' I whispered back.

'Oh,' he said, his serenity jolted. 'Well, um, take it easy.'

15

Written from Bertha's lodging, 397½ Dowling Street, Moore Park, dated Monday, 15 June 1903:

Harry,

Your letter has just come.

Your papers are not here. I looked for them before. There are also a good many of my private letters and papers missing, and I thought they may be amongst your things. Re the children. I will not consent to let them go. Not through any paltry feelings of revenge, but as a matter of duty. You see, you left me, with these two little children. I was turned into the world, with 1/6 and not a shelter or food for them. I had to pawn my wedding ring to pay for a room. And then had to leave the little children shut up in the room, while I sought for work. And when I got work to do I had to leave them all day, rush home to give them their meals. And back to work again. And mind you, I was suffering torture all the time with toothache, and had to tramp the cold wet streets all day, knowing unless I earnt some money that day the children would go hungry to bed. (I was a fortnight working before Robertson gave Miss [Rose] Scott that money.) I had no money to pay a dentist. (I wrote to you at P.A. Hospital telling you, you were forcing me to place the children in the Benevolent Asylum and you took no notice of the letter.) I went to the Dental Hospital and had a tooth extracted. They have broken part of the jaw bone. And I go into hospital on Wednesday and go under an operation to have the dead bone removed. The children will be well looked after. While I am away I have to pay a pound where they are going. So I trust you will endeavour to send Mr Henderson some more again this week. You know my condition and I am certainly not fit at the present moment to struggle for a living.

As far as the case goes, the sooner it is over the better. You alone have forced this step. God alone knows how often I have forgiven you and how hard I struggled for you. And how have you treated me. Harry there is no power on the earth will ever reunite us. You are dead to me as far as affection goes. The suffering I have been through lately has killed any thought of feeling I may have had for you.

When you have proved yourself a better man and not a *low drunkard* you shall see your children as often as you like. Until then, I will not let you see them. They have nearly forgotten the home scenes when you were drinking – and I will not let them see you drinking again. I train them to have the same love for you as they have for me. And if baby's prayers are heard in heaven, you should surely be different, to what you have been. They will have to decide the right and wrong between us, when they are old enough to understand. I think you are very cruel to

make the statements you do about me. You know Harry as well I
do they are absolutely false. Why don't you be a man. And if you
want to talk to people of your troubles, tell them *drink is the sole
cause.* Do not shield yourself behind a woman. Mr Henderson
cannot influence me one way or another, nor any one else. You
had your chance to sign a mutual separation and you would not
do it. I dread the court case and publicity more than you do. Still
I will not draw back again. And I only wish it was settled and
over to day. I am so weary of struggling against pain and sorrow
that I do not give a tinker's curse for anything – or anybody.

Bertha.[1]

Facts drift like the pollen on Dowling Street the day I visit. The
terraces are rusted and dusted by the constant traffic driving past.
One of them is undergoing renovation; through an open door you
can see new floorboards, a glossy fireplace and rickety steps to the
second floor.

Outside number 397, two plane trees have grown as tall as the
terrace, and the balcony has been walled in with glass. Next door,
the crucial fraction – 397½ – is written on the window above the
door.

The terrace Bertha brought the children to is now painted an
undercoat pink, with a green corrugated-iron balcony, windowed-
in like its neighbour. Plants entwine the security bars, and large
council garbage bins blight the entrance. Upstairs the tree branches
are reflected in the windowpanes. It was from inside here, beyond
today's sky-blue front door, that Bertha wrote an angry letter to
Henry about having to pawn her wedding ring and leave the children

shut up in her room while she looked for work. She warned of more proceedings, perhaps to continue to full dissolution of marriage.

Their daughter, Barta, later wrote that her mother was sometimes overly dramatic. Bertha's own mother lived in Sydney – surely that was an alternative to leaving them alone, or threatening to place them in the asylum? And what about her sister, Hilda?

But then conjecturing comes up against solid fact: *You know my condition.* Perhaps Bertha wasn't thinking at all about anything except survival.

I will not draw back again.

Still the facts keep drifting. In April 1903, the same month she filed her affidavit alleging cruelty and drunkenness, Bertha had written to Henry on the 23rd, saying that unless he sent money she would be forced to place the children 'in the Benevolent Asylum … I don't care about myself, but I cannot see my children starve … I think it is most dreadfully cruel for any Mother, to have to part with her children let alone be placed in the position that I am in.'[2] Initially it reads solely as financial but, having had two children, she must surely have suspected the significance of the missed periods, the swollen breasts, the heightened sense of smell that transforms the slightest scent into a stench. Or, perhaps, she tried to ignore them. There is no clear mention of a new baby in the letters until June.

The Benevolent Asylum's admissions and discharge ledger is an album of life stories, like this one on Wednesday 5 April 1903: 'Father Frederick sent to Gaol for four months for neglecting to support. Mother dead. Children committed by Newtown Police Court.'[3] It's fearful to look, then a relief to find that young Barta and Jim Lawson weren't there then.

In July, Bertha was clearer still: 'I am forced to write to you. I do not think you realize my position. I will be laid up either the end of October or first week in November ... There is the nurse to engage, and all my sewing to do, you know I have not any baby clothes.'[4]

Counting nine months back to summer from her due date – it was February, and they were still living in Manly when the *Critic* article gossiped that Mrs Lawson and Henry were sighted holding hands as they strolled around the beach cliffs. She must have conceived during this brief reunion. Now she warned Henry: 'I have to solely depend on you for an existance [*sic*] ... I cannot walk far or stand long ... You promised I should have every comfort. I am not asking you for that but for bare necessary's'.[5]

I remember in my own life a strange queasiness that was brought on by Dan blowing bubble gum. Then, on a horse ride one weekend away in country New South Wales, I inexplicably wanted to sleep in the sun by the reedy stream. Returning to Sydney, my period late, I did a pregnancy test. 'I better get a job,' Dan said.

Bertha might have blanched at food, but put her upset tummy down to stress. Realising that she was *with child* could have finally driven her to the lawyers, to pin down an agreement for continual support. But there was no mention of pregnancy enhancing her vulnerability in the April affidavit.

The baby is coming. The father is not. What do you do? Do you to try to reconcile again for the baby's sake? Or is it too late?

Too late.

⋏

Each word Bertha wrote feels like a clue: 'I think considering what Dr Brennand told you and after all your promises, it is most cruel that I should suffer all that agony again. If it were not for the sake of Jim and Bertha, I should not go through with it.'[6]

Did she mean that she would not go through with having the baby? Abortion was an open but illegal secret, especially in the bohemian world that Henry and Bertha inhabited. In a leather-bound report, *Royal Commission on the Decline of the Birth-Rate and the Mortality of Infants in New South Wales*, published in 1904, a witness told the Commission he had treated 150 women suffering from 'the effects of abortion' at his hospital.[7] Hannah Thornburn had died only the previous year, three days after she had collapsed from a feverish infection.

Despite his prominent Macquarie Street practice, Bertha's doctor, Henry Wolverine Brennand, was not one of the doctors, midwives, pharmacists, undertakers or religious witnesses who gave evidence to the Royal Commission that investigated the prevalence of abortion and contraceptive practices among women in New South Wales. These women and their midwives were, predictably, being blamed for the declining birth rate despite many being in Bertha's position, where they were reluctantly increasing it.

Bertha wrote to Henry of her pregnancy: 'it is not a very cheerful prospect to look forward to, knowing as you know well, I will very likely die.'[8] She sounds like she is being dramatic again, but pregnancy complications were dramatic in 1903.

Bertha may have given birth with a midwife at home, or at Crown Street Women's Hospital. Or she may have been helped by the Benevolent Society of New South Wales, who took in not only children but also destitute and single mothers at their 'lying in' wards. On today's flickering microfilm, those emotional lives are again compressed into crisp factlets, such as: 'Single. Pregnant. Alleged father. Emergency. Married. Deserted.'[9]

The only thing certain is that Bertha and Henry's last baby was stillborn sometime in late 1903. A nurse would have certified the stillbirth, and no other notification was required. This lack of birth or death registration was raised at the *Royal Commission on the Decline of the Birth-Rate and the Mortality of Infants in New South Wales*, because of its potential to conceal infanticide and midwifery negligence.

Bertha confirmed: 'the little one that we lost was born and the sad time came of our parting. For sorrow had come to us, and difficulties.'[10]

The sorrow.

16

Handwritten, to Henry from Bertha, dated 6 October 1906:

Dear Lawson

Re the amount to be paid by you for that children. I wish you would consider the matter seriously. It is impossible for me to keep them at Boarding School unless you pay the amount. I only ask you to pay for their Board as I manage their clothes, education, etc. ... [I] do not wish to have any more unpleasantness or court proceedings over the matter ... I have struggled hard enough the last three years and have kept the children well. But I find I cannot do it, and cannot face the worry. I have enough Business worries without the incessant anxiety of providing the necessary amount for the children's weekly account.

Trusting you will consider this matter in a proper light.

I remain yours etc.
B.L.[1]

The letters between Bertha and Henry disappear from the archives for three years. In her memoir, Bertha said proudly that she found work in this time at a little-known bookseller, Charles Stuart & Company. The company was listed as a 'Book importer and publisher' and registered in July 1903 at 42 Elizabeth Street, Sydney, so Bertha must have joined the firm in late 1903.

'I had been earning a living for myself and children as a sales-woman for Stuart and Co. ... As soon as I was well, I went back to this work, which was interesting and entailed much travelling, taking me all over New South Wales, and once, to New Zealand,' she wrote.[2]

It's unclear if her becoming 'well' is an oblique reference to her recovery from her stillbirth trauma, or her earlier 'rest' by the harbour in Manly that she says she had because of the stress in the lead-up to the separation. But she was well and working: not doing domestic work, which was the main sphere of employment for women at the turn of the century, but being engaged as a professional.

Imagine Bertha coming home from work, yawning. To care for the children while she was travelling away from Sydney, at first she must have relied on someone like Mrs Ellison, the 'very kind woman'[3] they had previously lived with at Manly after the separation, or perhaps her mother. Then she resorted to the expensive but reassuring solution of boarding school, but that appeared to have been unsustainable.

She wrote to Rose Scott in 1907 saying the children had whooping cough.[4] It flashes me back to when Ruby, despite being vaccinated, was infected as it flared up in Sydney. As the emergency doctors argued over whether she should be tested given she'd been immunised, she gasped deep distressing coughs into a hygiene mask. After the diagnosis was confirmed, I sent an email to her dad, with the subject 'Whooping Cough' – and a similar email another time, when she returned to Emergency with a broken wrist. These messages disappeared to wherever he was at the time. Through the flus and bugs of each season at her schools, I worked from home with her head on my lap.

'You should move home,' my father continued to insist, exasperated, when I saw him and his wife in the months after the separation. 'We can help you.'

I wonder if Bertha was told the same thing.

The prevailing narrative about Bertha is that she tried to rely on an unreliable husband, and punished him when he didn't provide. But that story's unfair. She is part of a new class of women – the working single mothers who are protected by the courts but pushed to the limit every day.

Henry remained living with Mrs Byers. There was a domestic peacefulness, and despite the frequent moves around the suburb to different homes, there was also a stability to which Henry always returned. 'It was Mrs Byers who gave the old-fashioned thing called friendship ... it was she who provided shelter and food for *her vagabond friend*,' author and family historian Olive Lawson said.[5]

I read Mrs Byers' more pleasant memories of Henry, as recorded by her biographer:

> Living in Euroka St, he made a great pet of a neighbour's dog. This dog was always on the look out for Lawson when he returned home and his bark was a signal to her to get ready

Lawson's evening meal and she knew almost exactly how long after this barking it would be before Lawson entered the house. Lawson always quietened the dog and gave it a homily on good manners ... 'What's the matter old chap? What's troubling you?' He'd reach the gate as happy as a child with all his troubles past. When his simple supper ended he was happy as a king ...

Whenever he was in a good mood, which was generally the case, he would ask her to sing him some old Ditty as he sat down to his tea. Sometimes when he was pleased with the ditty, he would say he had not heard it properly and ask her to sing it again into his hearing ear. At any line he liked, he would put up his hand and he would sing it for her himself with special emphasis on the part he liked. He never seemed to weary of hearing any good old Scottish tune.[6]

Henry, Bertha, Mrs Byers. It's another triangle of his life.

I meet with Mariana at her showroom. The wholesale fashion brand is in a street lined with mannequins in windows. Boxes of clothing wrapped in plastic surround her. Ruby browses through the racks of designs, half-listening.

After six months' separation, Mariana moved back from the beach cottage to the family home and her husband of 20 years. Then she left him again for a year, before returning and reuniting once more, but soon after this conversation she will leave him again – permanently. It's a pattern she acknowledges: 'It was for the children,' she says, and then pauses. 'It was our dream.'

The divorce for me was so certain. Yet love and loyalty tangle and strangle. Who am I to judge her for giving it another go? And a single mother is such an ironic description, because you are not single at all – you have a child or, like Mariana, four.

Ruby, still sorting through the clothes, hears as Mariana continues:

'When I left, it was a real uplifting feeling of "I finally did it". There was a wonderful feeling of totally having a say in your environment. I didn't have to put up with his cigarettes, although my son was smoking. I didn't have to deal with all the previous shit. But dealing with the children, and their needs, and working, was difficult. And that was just to pay bills. There was nothing left over. I didn't have it in me.

'There was no one supervising the kids. Because I was doing a job that was one-on-one, I had to be there for every minute of the money I earned. It was exhausting. I remember coming home, then I'd round up the kids – Sophia was only nine and roaming the suburb – and cook dinner. It was out of control. I found that impossible. My children were unsupervised. It didn't feel like it was going anywhere good.'

Her business partner joins our conversation: 'That's the situation for a lot of working mothers.' Mariana's partner isn't separated, but she's had long periods of sole parenting while her husband worked in China. 'I was working so many hours and the kids were catching the bus at all hours and Amy was coming home at ten years old and cooking. On their own, the kids were turning into little adults. You need an extended family.'

Mariana nods. 'There were the older children, but they didn't want to supervise. They were doing their own thing. I ended up with a massive blood disorder. I became unwell because I was so stressed out.' She turns to me: 'I remember thinking of you, that you did that for years. I think you found it so stressful and challenging to be working full-time, and looking after a child on your own.'

'I felt like I didn't do anything well,' I reply. I turn to Ruby: 'Do you remember what I was like, day to day?' I brace myself for what she will say.

'I just remember you – Mum – as Mum,' she says, with teenage bluntness. 'I remember childcare. Being the last to be picked up.'

'Sorry,' I tell her. I turn back to Mariana. 'I felt like Ruby was always missing out, or work was missing out …'

'It made you unwell,' Mariana says.

'Yes,' I say.

I remember the panic of trying to get to different childcare centres on time. Skidding down the school hill in the dark. Her head on my lap as I finished an interview. Dinners at a cheap Italian restaurant where we went so often after I picked her up that they knew her name and her favourite carbonara pasta. The blinding panic attacks that became as constant as the rushing around. The deep tiredness accompanied by wide-eyed nights. The gradual lack of interest in eating. The burning in my arms and my head.

And, always, a little girl.

The piano removalist takes off his jumper and his beer belly protrudes from his singlet. The other stocky man puts on thick gloves. The upright piano, played by Ruby's grandfather, then by her father, and now by Ruby herself, is chipped from many moves but, like our cat, it keeps surviving the change.

The first removalist nods, and the other levers the piano from the truck. They have blue straps ready on their shoulders to haul it up two flights of stairs.

'How much does a piano weigh?' I ask, then realise it's probably not the time to remind him.

'A few hundred kilos,' he replies.

'Should have married a guitarist,' I say.

The piano is the heaviest reminder of her father that Ruby brings to each new flat. Soon after the separation, we had moved to the harbourside suburb of McMahons Point, to be closer to my work. I had transferred her to a school close by too, so everything was within walking distance. Ruby and I had our own triangle of life, with this piano at its core.

Faced with the cost and the stairs, I initially offered it to a family friend, but Ruby was so bereft that I reneged and it was duly hauled up the 20-odd stone steps. After it was heaved into place, Ruby sat down, settled at the stool and tested out each key, and began to play.

Coincidentally, our apartment was close to where Henry lived with Mrs Byers at scattered residences through McMahons Point and neighbouring Waverton. He also lived among the area's pubs, which were his court. His observant eye was still clear and perceptive, chronicling pain and loss, especially at the bar. But bitterness was sounding too, just like the tones outside the Family Court, of stricken, seething whispers in huddles with lawyers. Henry wrote:

> Our pub ... is a small hotel on the top of a cliff with a view across a small bay, of almost the only bit of real bush headland left in the city's heart. It is frequented – haunted – by ancient mariners, wharf and waterside characters, carters, casual smugglers and such like – and, strange to say, by a few ghosts of retired and forgotten bushmen. There are likewise a disbarred solicitor – an artist in somewhat the same domestic boat as the struck-off gent;– a very cheerful professor of something or

other – now he's called 'The Pro,' and one or two other improper persons of the like – to say nothing of one known as 'the Pote' behind his back, and 'Arry to his face.

We of the pub are mostly separated from our wives, and anything else (except beer) that makes life interesting. In certain stages of our sprees, which last through weeks, all women are either soulless or fiends with the tongues of hell-hags. In other words our wives are, or were, all *Noble Women.*[7]

Later, as the rent increased, we moved to a one-bedroom-and-studio apartment that was squashed among the skyscrapers but still close to school and work. The shared rooftop was Ruby's playground, and we also walked to the park or the pool, through streets in which Henry lived. When that place became too cramped, we moved to a bigger apartment and rented the sunroom to a boarder.

'Move,' my dad continued to plead, exasperated. 'We can help you here.'

'Ruby is happy in her school. She has friends,' I said, determined. In truth, she can make friends anywhere. She is resilient, mobile. She is part of a generation who has parents in two residences, if not countries. And it seemed like a failure to move home. It felt like I'd be giving up.

Now, living on the other side of the Harbour Bridge, I return on a winter night to McMahons Point. I'm meeting with a friend, a former colleague, at one of Henry's pubs, now called The Blues Point Hotel. We are Noble Women among groups of men dressed variously in suits and high-vis jackets, smoking on the terrace. The pub was rebuilt after Henry's time, has changed names and, like life, is in constant renovation. The last time I was here was with work. we'd have long lunches or watch the Melbourne Cup. As the hours passed, I'd keep my eye on the clock to make sure I'd be able to pick Ruby up from after-school care. Now the wooden bar and beer-stained floor have been replaced by shiny silver shelves and an open area covered by blue-and-white carpet. A framed photo of the old ferry wharf is a small homage to the past. Despite this forced elegance, it still feels like a blokey pub, where men can group around the large-screen TV, have a beer and talk about 'Noble Women'.

An old neighbour, a retired academic, is at the bar and asks how my work is going.

'Writing about Henry Lawson,' I say. 'This was one of his pubs, wasn't it?'

'Yes, he drank here,' he confirms. 'Have you seen his seat?'

'Here?' I ask, looking around.

'No. Further up the hill.'

My friend waves me over.

'Look at it,' my old neighbour says, going back to his table.

We order vodka and chips; my friend has brought another colleague and we bond over exes, comparing where they are.

'Caribbean,' I say of Dan. 'And I have an ex in France. Possibly. He's a travel writer.'

'Dubai, Paris,' she ticks off.

Later that night I hail a taxi, too tired to take two trains home. As we accelerate up the hill, I see a stone seat with a plaque. It blurs behind us.

Excerpts from Henry Lawson's 'To Jim', which was included in his
When I Was King and Other Verses, 1905:

> I gaze upon my son once more,
>   With eyes and heart that tire,
> As solemnly he stands before
>   The screen drawn round the fire;
> With hands behind clasped hand in hand,
>   Now loosely and now fast –
> Just as his fathers used to stand
>   For generations past …
>
> These lines I write with bitter tears
>   And failing heart and hand,
> But you will read in after years,
>   And you will understand:
> You'll hear the slander of the crowd,

They'll whisper tales of shame,
But days will come when you'll be proud
To bear your father's name.[1]

Henry also wrote a poem entitled 'Barta', published in 1903:

Wide solemn eyes that question me,
Wee hand that pats my head –
Where only two have stroked before,
And both of them are dead.
'Ah, poo-ah Daddy mine,' she says,
With wondrous sympathy –
Oh, baby girl, you don't know how
You break the heart in me! …

But one shall love me while I live
And soothe my troubled head,
And never hear an unkind word
Of me when I am dead.
Her eyes shall light to hear my name
Howe'er disgraced it be –
Ah, baby girl, you don't know how
You help the heart in me![2]

The kiddies. Bertha's letters, at least those in the later years, show that the children missed Henry, and wanted him. She wavered between protecting the children and promoting their relationship. She wavered a lot. *Henry, are you yourself?* It is code for drinking.

Barta later recalled a day when she was small and they met Henry on a tram. After it rattled around the cliffs they went for a picnic on the rocks at the Spit.

> When I think of my memories of Dad, there are so very few. My first meeting with him appears to be on the back of an old Spit tram. At least, that's when I first clearly remember him. He seemed very tall, and was dressed in comfortable old clothes, and he got on a stop or two after we did. He had a large cane picnic hamper, the square sort with the skewered lid. He sat this on the floor and took me on his knee ...
>
> We were making for the tiny beach on the other side of Middle Harbour, a little rocky curve long buried under the highway. He had brought chicken, and some other treat for Jim and I. He loved to be responsible for the day's outing. I remember I was busily exploring some rocks, while Mother bathed and Jim went wandering off, and I fell in. My wails brought Dad flying. I had cut my foot, not badly, but I remember how upset he was, tearing a handkerchief into strips and binding it firmly while he comforted and quieted me.[3]

She remembered too 'how carefully he would brush his moustache aside when he stooped to kiss me'.[4] Their family outing – nuclear, secure – by the time she wrote this down had been packed up as a memory. Barta also recalled Henry visiting them at their Walker Street home, which Bertha had moved to sometime in the previous three years. Henry was there on the periphery of their lives. According to his letters, he was just around the corner with Mrs Byers. There were times – interspersed with the intense hostility, the drunkenness – when it seems they tried to be a family.

What did Bertha remember of those days? How did she feel when she saw other picnicking families packing up their baskets and leaving together? Did these families upset her? Did she, when Henry was elsewhere, feel envy like I did, when she saw fathers with their children curled securely in their arms, and the dog trotting beside them? Or was she cynical, like I sometimes was too, knowing that the veneer of family life is fragile?

Barta was three at the time of the separation, and she had previously been separated from her mother while Bertha was hospitalised in London. Jim was five. In those early years, there's always acceptance by children of what is.

'I didn't understand it until I was older, until I was ten or something,' Ruby told me in Mariana's shop. 'I don't remember a change – Dad was always away, so it wasn't different.'

Ruby lives in a world in which her friends also have divorced parents, but how did Barta and Jim feel? Perhaps they were protected by Bertha's judicial separation. They could continue to say 'My parents are still married' if someone dared ask, even though legally it was a separation ratified by the dreaded Divorce Court.

Barta remembered a father more than a divorce:

> Dad was tall, tense, straight. He had marvellous eyes. You could go on looking down and down in them. He liked to dress in a slightly old fashioned way. He wore dignified high collars and he was never without his stick. He was a far more powerful personality than any sentimental dreaming could make of him. He was a law unto himself, and often difficult, but just as often warm and friendly, full of laughter, kindness and quick understanding, as he always was with us.

147

He had a gleeful sense of the absurd ... He spoke softly. He was quiet and he could be very gentle. He could be restless, nervously impatient rearing as a thoroughbred, very angry at anything he thought was blind unfairness, but just as ready with sorrow and apology.[5]

Because of his recurring child-support debts, it is easy to dismiss Henry as an uncaring father, just as dismissing Bertha as the bitch might seem like an answer. Bertha tried to be diplomatic in public, even if her letters demanded money and pleaded for him to see the children. It seems that he was around; it's just that you aren't sure when, or where. She wrote: 'Harry did come to see us – at heart he was a good husband and father, except when the temptation to drink was too strong.'[6]

There is a lost narrative here of Henry as a separated father. In 'To Jim', the lyrical lines reveal his anxiety about his future relationship with the boy, and there's sad sweetness for his daughter in the poem 'Barta'. He'd pleaded with his wife that she at least let him see little Barta, in a letter written as the separation spiralled to court.

Barta always had her memories of a father showing love to his children with sporadic, spontaneous generosity – a doll instead of boring necessities – so much more memorable than the cost of living, which so consumed her mother.

I remember Dan arriving with a giant pink stuffed unicorn that sprawled across Ruby's bed. 'Guilt present,' his sister observed.

Sometimes Henry came with just his humour and intellect, and helped with schoolwork, and that seems to be remembered most vividly of all.

In the Mitchell Library, the Lawson family archival boxes are crammed with Barta's letters to her mother, with notes about her parents and with recollections that reveal the reality she later saw, in contrast with what she wanted to see as a child who loved both her parents.

All divorced parents know that their children will eventually have their own contested versions to tell. Few are left in libraries.

18

Excerpts from 'One Hundred and Three', composed in 1908:

With the frame of a man, and the face of a boy, and a
    manner strangely wild,
And the great, wide, wondering innocent eyes of a
    silent-suffering child,
With his hideous dress and his heavy boots, he drags to
    Eternity –
And the Warder says, in a softened tone: 'Keep step,
    One Hundred and Three' …

They shut a man in the four-by-eight, with a six-inch slit
    for air,
Twenty-three hours of the twenty-four, to brood on his
    virtues there.
And the dead stone walls and the iron door close in as
    an iron band

On eyes that followed the distant haze far out on the
level land.

Bread and water and hominy, and a scrag of meat and a
spud,
A Bible and thin flat book of rules, to cool a strong
man's blood;
They take the spoon from the cell at night – and a
stranger might think it odd;
But a man might sharpen it on the floor, and go to his
own Great God.

One Hundred and Three, it is hard to believe that you
saddled your horse at dawn;
There were girls that rode through the bush at eve, and
girls who lolled on the lawn.
There were picnic parties in sunny bays, and ships on
the shining sea;
There were foreign ports in the glorious days – (Hold
up, One Hundred and Three!) …

The great, round church with its volume of sound,
where we dare not turn our eyes –
They take us there from our separate hells to sing of
Paradise.
In all the creeds there is hope and doubt, but of this
there is no doubt:
That starving prisoners faint in church, and the warders
carry them out.[1]

Rushing, always rushing. I climb the curling stone stairs, taking my shoes off as I go, and hurry across the chapel to a makeshift canvas tent. A moment later, I'm ready.

Sun spills through the chapel's upper windows, striping the wooden floor. 'Sorry I'm late,' I say to the life-drawing tutor. 'Traffic.'

'It happens.'

'Hair up or down?' I ask.

'Up,' he says.

I knot my hair into a rough bun. Hair obscures bone structure.

The others in the room chat and yawn. I keep the kimono knotted. Students at the National Art School, they concentrate on their pencils, their charcoal and their coffee. I stare at the sandstone. It's not personal, just protocol. The model must not be approached by students, nor photographed, nor treated disrespectfully. The model in turn must not walk around in the nude unnecessarily.

The tutor nods. I am a living sculpture who was late.

I untie the sash of the white kimono and drop the gown to the floor. It lies in a crumpled pool of discarded modesty. I stand still, one arm behind my back, my head down, feeling the nearby heater on my toes.

The students pick up their pencils and point them at my body. They frown and squint. They scrutinise my breast, analyse my thigh and assess my bottom.

I breathe, counting the seconds. At 60, I turn to the left. A rustle of paper means the students have turned with me. Fast drawings are supposed to capture the essence of the body.

Three minutes.

I look up.

Prior to the National Art School, the chapel was part of Darlinghurst Gaol. A jagged line scars the sandstone wall, marking the former mezzanine level on which the female prisoners assembled for prayer, their notes fluttering down to the men below while a soprano convicted of infanticide sang hymns.[2] Poet and prisoner Henry Lawson wrote about the chapel in his poem 'One Hundred and Three'.

The tutor nods again. He wants another pose.

My head turns to the front. I stare at the stained-glass windows, glowing with the morning light. They were created by the convicted bushranger Frank Pearson and the 'Demon Dentist' Henry Bertrand. The windows depict the parables of the lost coin, the prodigal son and the lost sheep. With my hands clasped across my legs, I read the abridged inscription stained into the glass: 'I say unto you that likewise joy shall be in heaven over one sinner that repenteth more than over ninety and nine just persons which need no repentance.'[3]

I breathe, stand still and gaze at redemption.

After our separation, I registered with the Child Support Agency to receive parenting payments. I am fortunate to live in an era that recognises single parents' needs, although there is constant debate about the amount I'm entitled to. I'd found a job as a part-time journalist; supplemented by art modelling and the odd freelance article, plus help from my mother and, later, my partner, this meant I was not totally reliant on the government or on my gypsy ex.

The CSA officer did his best. 'Where is your husband?' he asked.

'The Caribbean, I think,' I said. 'He travels around.' Whenever Ruby asked, usually I took a stab at the approximate region.

'I'll check if we have reciprocal agreements there.' He returned, pleased. 'Barbados? Is he there?'

'Sometimes,' I said, trying to be helpful too.

'Florida? We have a reciprocal arrangement with the USA ...'

'I'd like to have a regular payment from him, but his earnings are all over the place and he travels all the time ... He's a musician.'

'Oh,' he said. 'A musician.'

He seemed genuinely concerned about my daughter's welfare. I was surprised, thinking that hearing parents complain and protest day after day would jade you. But he and I both knew reciprocal agreements were complicated and difficult to enforce. As tempting as it was to enforce a regular payment for budgeting, as Bertha had needed to do, I knew that, until Dan was actually living in one place for an extended time, the amount that would be imposed wouldn't be worth the difficulty of obtaining it under the various international jurisdictions. And all that would flow from this effort would be resentment rather than money. It wasn't practical, given the situation.

Nevertheless, the CSA officer asked for estimates of income for both of us, so he could calculate the minimal amount of child support that Dan should be paying. When his estimate finally arrived in the post, I glanced at it and then threw it on my pile of bills.

Rain hits Sydney with a three-day storm. A woman sits in a rail tunnel hunched on a milk crate, with a styrofoam cup and a hand-scrawled sign lying on the tiles in front of her: I'M HOMELESS DUE TO DOMESTIC VIOLENCE. I'M SIX MONTHS PREGNANT. I'VE BEEN ON THE STREETS FOR THE LAST FEW NIGHTS AND I'M PETRIFIED.

There have been more and more homeless women around the city since refuges recently closed after a government funding cut. Her stomach bulges over grey trackpants spotted with dirt. 'I've been trying all these places,' she says. 'They are all full because of the storm, or they are just full ...' She can't try anymore because her phone was stolen on the streets. She borrows my phone and calls another refuge. She looks exhausted. Happy-face tattoos decorate her arms.

Imagine Bertha's mother whispering as my mother often did to me in those first few years, 'Do you need money, love?' Bertha's sister perhaps quietly opening her purse with gloved hands to give her some shillings. And Bertha taking them with an embarrassed thanks, or a snappy no, or a grateful hug – depending on her pride and her mood.

'Why do you think Bertha was so unpopular?' my partner asks. As a history buff, and in the midst of a divorce himself after a long separation, he is interested in my research.

'I don't know if Bertha had a choice. They had no money. The bailiffs came all the time. Henry was an alcoholic. Whereas Hilda, the sister … there was money.' Enough, it seems, to support two homes in Sydney – one for their family, and one for her husband's mistress and their son. There's a later picture of Hilda – confident, blond and wearing a fur coat, the wife of Premier Jack Lang, the most important man in the state. Her husband's son came to live with them after his mother's death and was absorbed into the family.

Without family and her work, how much worse off would Bertha have been? How much worse off would Ruby and I have been without the support of family? They not only helped me financially, supplementing Dan's sporadic generosity, but they supported me in everyday life.

Lives unravel. You recover, but it takes time. The sense of vulnerability remains; the sense of responsibility is always there. Familiar feelings return unexpectedly, irrationally.

'I have to make sure I can look after you,' I told my daughter recently. She reached for my hand.

Bertha's letters to Henry feel familiar. As she tried various tactics in asking for money, she called him 'dearie', 'Harry', 'Henry', 'Lawson'; but when letters were from her lawyer, the detachment kicked in: 'Sir'.

I look back through some emails I sent to Dan, far back in my Sent box. Like Bertha's letters, mine range from polite to pissed off: *I can deal with living expenses but bills like this are really hard ... can you send me that money ... I've already borrowed off Mum. I haven't got any money after paying for everything ... I have $70 after paying the rent until I get paid ... I only have $100 until I get paid, and out of that I have to pay for Ruby's excursion ($25) ... I'm not earning enough to make ends meet ... I know you are in the Caribbean somewhere, surely there is a bank ... Are you still in London, I need you...*

Dan always answered from somewhere. He was by turns flush and frugal: *Sure. I hope this helps a little ... I sent you $ to get out of a scrape ... I want to help you out, things have been tight for me too ...*

It's the same tone, the same words, just a different method of communication.

The anxiety. The exhaustion. The lack.

A friend lives in a blue-painted house, with a landscaped pond and vegetable garden, that she has renovated herself. It gleams with care. She has a boarder, but her home is paid off and her daughter now has children of her own.

When her husband left, their daughter was four and this was just a rundown cottage.

'I bought him out,' she says. 'My mother helped. I did all this later.'

We eat under a tree by her pond, a small palm frond flapping over the table in the afternoon wind.

'We had a private agreement for support – the Child Support Agency hadn't started yet. It was hard. I was living on casual earnings. I felt I was bringing her up in a slum. The wind blew through holes in the windows.

'During that time, he said he had no money. He wasn't paying anything. He came to our house and saw the holes, her broken trampoline and knew she slept in my old single bed on a lumpy mattress. And he said, "I have no money." I said, "Please. Just $20 a week." He said yes, and then he rang me and said, "I'm not paying for your lifestyle." What fucking lifestyle? Bringing up a four-year-old in deep poverty?'

I remember what Bertha wrote to Henry: 'it does not look as "If I were one of the most extravagant women" does it!'[4]

My friend continues: 'He said, "I'm not a monster." He was so angry. I said, "I'm not the one saying that. Do you think you are a monster?"

'He kept saying, "I can't afford it." So, after seven years, I took him to court in December and subpoenaed his income. He said, "I got your Christmas present." I found out he'd been earning $89,000 a year, and this was 30 years ago. I was white hot with anger. I said, "You are beneath contempt. Don't step foot in my house again." But I never stopped him seeing our daughter.'

Later that day, she drops me at the train station. She is still talking: 'People say, "You should be over it." I can forgive human nature. But to let his daughter suffer in poverty when he could have helped? That's unforgivable. He's not an appalling man – he's a weak man.'

She hugs me goodbye, a pocket rocket of resilience.

I read that almost one in three of persistently jobless families are headed by single parents.[5] One of my friends, formerly a single parent, is a successful psychologist with a brass shingle outside her office building. Another one has paid off her home. Julia Ross, whom I once interviewed, found out like Bertha that she was pregnant soon after separating from her partner – and sold everything to start her own HR consultancy. She later listed it on the stock exchange and bought a $21 million home in which to raise her son. 'I only wanted to give my baby a secure education and future,' she said.

The cracks in society into which single parents fall are sometimes shallow; but for the majority, the cracks are wide and deep.

I remember a conversation with my partner at a restaurant. When Ruby is 15, the three of us decide to live together as a family. He pays for rent, designer shoes and dinners that are at odds with my bank balance. He gave Ruby a computer. And because the piano, finally, wouldn't make it up more flights of stairs, he gave her a keyboard, too.

But loyalties and independence clash. I'm both grateful and resistant. I am determined to look after Ruby; she's my responsibility, and, as my partner reminds me, her father's.

At the table, with thick white napkins spread across our laps, he asks, 'Has he given you any money?'

'No,' I say. Our private, if sporadic, agreement of the past – in which Dan helped whenever he signed up for a cruise – broke down. 'He says work is slow and that he hasn't got any at the moment – he's living on credit. But he's in America now. If it doesn't happen soon, I'm going to Child Support again.'

I remember that conversation about reciprocal agreements with the Child Support officer soon after we split; it seemed pointless at the time.

'What will that do?' he asks, blunt as a butter knife. 'You'll get hardly anything.'

'It will be something,' I insist. 'It's the principle.'

'You're like Bertha,' he says. 'Going after him for the *principle*. She was obsessed.'

'Obsessed?' I repeat. I've lost my appetite. 'What is obsessive about supporting your child? Maybe she was obsessed with trying to find a way to stop feeling so stressed about money. She needed him to help.'

'She fixated. Henry didn't have any money. His friends had to help. She was ill, wasn't she?'

'It's not about her illness. And he was ill too. That's a separate issue to supporting your kids. Why shouldn't he support his children?'

'You misunderstand,' he says. 'It's not just about money. It's the emotional support too. Going to Child Support won't fix that.'

I look out the window at the water view. 'I can't remember how we got onto this subject.'

'You're upset,' he says.

Soon after this, Dan texts in the middle of the night to say that he is unable to get to a bank, because he is in port on a Sunday, but he's wired money. I can pick it up.

'Tell Ruby I love her,' he adds. 'I'll start paying something every month while I'm on this contract.' I remember what Bertha said. *At heart, he was a good father.*

I look up locations for Moneygram and find 7-Elevens and exchange booths in shopping malls all over the city. I've done this many times over the preceding years. I grab my passport and line up with the tourists and travellers.

I give the cashier the reference number and my identification. She hands me a form with multiple translations of the questions. As I fill it out, she looks at the computer and at my passport, and back again.

'Do you have any other identification with your name on it?' she asks.

'You have my passport.'

'The sender hasn't put your full name,' she explains. 'I need something that matches the name on the sender's form.'

'What's he put?' I ask. I think of his nicknames for me over the years. Kez? Bloss? I doubt it.

She shows me. My middle name, which appears on my passport and licence, is missing.

'He's my ex-husband,' I explain through the glass. 'He's probably forgotten what my middle name is. You have my photo ID.' And I show her the text with the receiver number.

The tourists behind me shift in the queue to the other cashier. An older traveller strides off.

She talks to a manager in a side room, and then calls Moneygram. She hangs up and says to me: 'Sorry. They say no unless the names match.'

'It will take weeks for him to do it again.' I insist. 'It's for my daughter's music tutor.'

My partner hovers, concerned and annoyed Dan hasn't discovered bank transfers like everyone else. 'I'll give you the money until it comes,' he placates. 'It's okay.'

But I'm sick of asking. It's all exhausting.

Is this how Bertha felt?

19

To David Scott Mitchell, written at Angus & Robertson's Sydney Book Club library, circa 6 April 1905:

Dear Mr Mitchell,

Have been separated for two years. I had a bad attack two months ago and went to the Receiving House. On my discharge I received a summons for £6 12s. and last Monday week was sent to Darlinghurst Gaol. On my release, I am served with the appended summons. Can you help me to meet it? I have been working. I have been drinking lately, but I *never* ill-treated my wife, and I kept her in comfort. This is the fourth separation and it is a most shameful and cruel case for all parties concerned. *I intend to defend the next action.*

Yours truly,
Henry Lawson[1]

It's been raining. The glare gives the palm trees a neon shine and wet jacaranda blossoms smear onto the gravel. The National Art School's gates are flung open for the crowd streaming in.

It's hot in the twilight. We take glasses and stand among the throng. Artists mingle with the cultured alcoholics – well-dressed regulars at every art event that offers a bar – who hover for refills, like a modern-day Dawn and Dusk Club.

Imagine Henry here in another life, clutching his beer and dogged by an uneasy déjà-vu as he looks around at the high sandstone walls that caged him sporadically between 1905 and 1909 for defaulting on his child support. *Keep step, One Hundred and Three!*

Later we leave through the Burton Street gates, pausing at the entry to a small sandstone building that is guarded by a skull, an hourglass and another strange symbol carved into the stone. It used to be the mortuary but is now the electricity room for the school. We leave it glowing with light and death, and move into the night.

After the divorce laws were first enacted in the 1870s, the Benevolent Society's president, Sir Arthur Renwick, advocated enforcing maintenance payments for deserted wives and children, because he saw so many destitute mothers at the Society's charitable doors. He had an elaborate moustache, like Henry's, and kind eyes that transcend the stiffness of his photograph.

And by 1905, the divorce laws did indeed support women to some degree, at least for the children. Sections 42 and 43 of the *Matrimonial Causes Act 1899* decreed a traditional, brutal form of enforcing child support, for a maximum of 12 months' imprisonment:

42. Where the application for judicial separation is by the wife the Court may make any order for alimony which it deems just.

43. Where a decree is made for judicial separation the Court may make all such orders in respect of alimony to the wife as it could make if the decree made was for dissolution of marriage.[2]

Henry wasn't alone in his situation. In a sketch about men in gaol for not paying support, Henry wrote:

> They are 'up for maintenance' (one for neglecting to keep his alleged wife, and the other his alleged child). One has been fined double the amount in arrears, or three months. The other has been ordered to be detained in Darlinghurst Gaol until the amount is paid. The first is sure to be out in three months, and then have worked off his fine and also the amount of the 'arrears'; the other expects friends to pay up in a few days, but if they don't, he might be there for twelve months and 'arrears' running on all the time. Then his only hope will be to get clear of the Commonwealth and female suffrage in the fortnight's grace they'll give him when he does get out. Both prisoner and 'confinee' wish that women were never invented, and as they become confidential, they grow quite warm on the subject of matrimony.[3]

The year before he wrote this, Henry – through the character of the older bushman Bob – in his 'Triangles of Life' summed up the life that had led him to Darlinghurst Gaol in this condensed way:

I. Childhood: Rows and scenes and scenes and rows, violent rows that frightened; mother and father separated; home a hell. Boy slavery and freedom.

II. Cheap boarding house, pretty, but hysterical, daughter; mother, step-father, and sisters; rows and scenes more violent than at home. Tale of ill-treatment. Last big row. Cab, box, and hurried, mad marriage at a 'matrimonial bureau'. Seven years of it.

III. Police court. Desertion. 'Judicial separation'. Maintenance order. Reconciliation – court – reconciliation – court. Summons for desertion, and maintenance. Summons, summons, summons, Darlinghurst. And the full knowledge of what sort of woman she was.[4]

Passing outside the high walls of the one-time Darlinghurst Gaol, on my way home from work, I touch the sandstone. It feels cold.

From inside here, Henry Lawson wrote to his book publisher, George Robertson, on 27 August 1908:

Dear Robertson,

I want you to read this letter. I did not waste a shilling of that £5, but paid it where it was long due and sorely needed (a grocer in North Sydney, crippled with rheumatism and his wife about to be confined). Mrs Byers can tell you this. I thought I would be alright. I thought I would be able to finish a story and some verses I had on hand, but I was hunted too much. I was sober when brought here, and sober the day before. I gave myself up, when things seemed hopeless, to get a sleep. I am sending Mrs Byers to see you this morning. She will tell you what she has done, and what money she has got.

I have been here three weeks and it is more than enough. I was three days under separate treatment, and then on the works, but broke down and was brought from the cell into the hospital out of my mind. If I am not released I shall have to go back to the cells again, and that will spell *finis* as far as my brain is concerned …

We are not allowed to write here and will not be allowed to smoke for six months (except when ordered by the doctor in the hospital). It is the waste of time that is killing me now … the horror of the place is on me this time, and was before I came in. I never experienced cells before. Think and imagine the effect of such confinement on a temperament like mine …

And, I understand, the maintenance order will go on, or be in operation all the time I am rotting in idleness here … I am not writing this because I am on the wrong side of the bars, but I'm done with the drink for twelve months at the very least after I get out. I made up my mind to that three weeks ago. I kept it for two years, last, you know, through seas of trouble …

And, remember those verses of mine
'When a man's in a hole you must send round the hat,
Were he gaol-bird or gentleman once.'
… Do your best to get me out of this and into the sunlight without delay and you will never regret it.

Yours truly,
Henry Lawson

I would agree to any conditions and keep them.

Have been letting my beard grow, and it's white underneath.

Gave me quite a shock.[5]

The National Art School courtyard is quiet when the students are in class. The sandstone buildings were converted in the 1920s from Darlinghurst Gaol to a technical college. Now it's this peaceful art school, under a grey sky streaked with sunlight. Palm trees shade the seats and fringe the hangout cafe. A white-shirted security officer strolls with a walkie-talkie in his pocket.

Today archivist Deborah Beck meets me. The author of *Hope in Hell: A History of Darlinghurst Gaol and the National Art School*, she's immersed in the characters once incarcerated here. She recites the names of bushrangers: 'Captain Thunderbolt, Captain Moonlite …' And in 1882, JF Archibald himself was imprisoned here, for failing to pay the court costs resulting from a libel action against *The Bulletin*.

By 1905 when Henry began begging his benefactors and editors for help, Archibald was mentally imprisoned by anxiety. He was no longer in a position to help Henry. He had been committed to Callan Park Hospital for the Insane, which, like the former Darlinghurst Gaol, has served as an art school campus, for the University of Sydney. Patients who once lived there still sometimes wander into the buildings, unsure where they now belong.

The building across the courtyard, like the others, is rounded, built from sandstone and renovated. The art shop spills merchandise outside a side entrance. Inside, Deborah leads me down some stairs into a dim lower passage lined with doors. Stretching her arms out, she touches both walls with her hands. I can easily touch the ceiling.

'When I do tours, I talk about Lawson here,' she says. 'This is closest to what he describes the cell as – a sandstone tomb. Look at the stone roof, and the width of the walls. Single cells were eight feet by five feet and ten feet high.' I calculate the metric equivalents. Two and a half metres long, one and a half metres wide and three metres high. A lanky man like Henry could only pace a few steps.

A rusted, iron-barred gate leans against a claustrophobic arch. 'I think that's where the clothes were distributed,' Deborah observes of the tiny space within. A picture on the wall shows prison garb, which is surprisingly civilised, with brimmed hats and waistcoats. Almost hipster. 'In his gaol photos, Henry wore a suit. They dressed in almost street clothes.'

Deborah explains that after the new prisoners – whether a poet who owed pounds to his wife, or a wife killer – were brought through the gates, they were led down here to this dark passage, under the Governor's Quarters. They were checked by the doctor and given prison clothes; they surrendered their personal belongings.

We move further down the tunnel and she opens a door, revealing stairs to what was the men's bathhouse. She points out some blue mottling on the sandstone, like bluebottles on a beach: 'That's the original colour of the gaol. Blue was supposed to calm, but I think personally all it did was make them feel cold.'

'He wrote about the cold,' I remember. 'He said it was never warm, even on a summer's night …'[6]

'His writing is the best description of the gaol,' says Deborah. 'Other writing is formal descriptions from officials, but his is lyrical.'

Up the stairs, the dimness gives way to the morning sun, and we're in a building adjoining the cafe. 'It's impossible to know where he was exactly but, because it was alimony, this was the debtors' quarter.' She turns around, gesturing to another building close by, now the NAS Gallery. 'He may have also been in there, because he describes the staircase.'

This was where the tougher criminals were sent. *It is real gaol – grim gaol this time.*[7]

Out of the debtors' quarter, we go back into the main courtyard. 'Then he got solitary confinement for writing poems for other prisoners. The murderer George Love stole a pencil and paper from the printer for him. It was a terrible thing to be put in solitary for. It was dark for 23 hours a day … It was too harsh.'

Throughout his sporadic incarcerations, Henry pleaded against the harshness to his friends, begging for help to meet the debt and railing against Bertha. In an earlier gaoling during 1906, he entreated Magistrate Francis Sheriff Isaacs for relief, protesting that he wasn't drinking but he'd been recently put into Darlinghurst Gaol and had 'got the kids fixed up for twelve months ahead' so, as a result, was 'very hard up' and 'the wife is thoroughly bad'.[8] Given the tone of this letter, I'm reading 'bad' as *bitch*.

In the same bitter letter, Henry claimed Bertha was travelling 'saloon passage' to Perth and claimed his trouble was because of her 'secret gambling'. But the comfortable travel may have been paid for by her company, as she was by now a sales representative for Stuart and Co. The gambling is a curve ball. In biographies of Henry, Bertha's been called callous, and vengeful and mad, but the only gamble was in marrying Henry.

I think of Henry in his sandstone tomb. For all Henry's faults and defaults, I don't think Bertha would have wanted him like this, desperate in the dark.

20

Letter by Prisoner 32, to Mrs Byers, dated 26 September 1909:

Dear Mrs Byers,

I have had a heavy cold and my head is not clear, so must write anyhow ... I think we can only write on Sunday, and I only have got two letters ...

The case seems desperate, but do all you possibly can. I'd soon go hopelessly out of my mind here. Do anything to raise the money, and I'll take care this business will never happen again. You might go even to my mother. She has plenty. Her address is Mrs Lawson, 'Old Stone House', Tempe (near Railway Station) ... Her property is near the railway gates. She'd tell you of some friends anyway. It is real gaol this time, you know, and the loneliness is terrible ...

Yours in trouble,
Henry Lawson[1]

✶

Across the courtyard in the Art School's library, once Darlinghurst Gaol's hospital, there are aisles of art books and an enclosed verandah overlooking the school.

'He was at the hospital a lot,' Deborah Beck tells me. 'He would have walked here for exercise. I think about what he would have seen. The view would have been the same, except for fewer trees. And they've taken the bars away that used to be over the windows.'

In her book, Deborah writes about Henry befriending murderer David Hanna in the hospital walkways. Hanna's trial was reported throughout May 1903, the same year Henry and Bertha separated. Using Hanna's wife's deathbed testimony, the court heard what happened on the night of the murder, which took place in the couple's laundrette:

> the prisoner came home about 4 o'clock in the afternoon. He then said he wanted his dinner. His wife said, 'It is a very busy day ... Go down to Webster's and get some dinner.' He was then a little bit abusive ... He began to talk about divorce cases, and he said, 'I will go out and buy a revolver, and I will blow your brains out.' She said, 'Oh, that's all right.' ... He then went out again, and when he came back, about 9 o'clock, he was more abusive than ever ... Things went on in this way till shortly after 11 o'clock ... He then went up to her with the revolver in his hand, and he said, 'Come into the room and shut the door.' She refused. He said, 'Who's the boss here?' She said, 'As far as the door is concerned, I am.' He then fired at her.[2]

Witnesses heard a second shot, which Hanna had aimed at himself.

Henry recalled walking for hours in the corridor of the barred hospital with Hanna, who was

> under sentence of death and had a separate table at meals. He was suffering from an old bullet wound in the head. He said he was sorry she died. He told me all about it: cackling, mischief making women neighbours and relatives invading his home – and all. I sympathised with that man – his trouble had been in some respects so like my own.[3]

From the old hospital corridor, now the verandah with the bars removed, there is a clear view of the sandstone and courtyard below. We're quiet, with Henry in our thoughts.

'What do you think of Bertha?' I ask Deborah. 'She was seen as the bitch, although she had her supporters too.'

Deborah considers this. 'She had to survive, and she had two children. It was harder to work then with kids. It seems harsh, but I understand it as well.'

I try with difficulty to remain balanced when Henry comes up in conversation. My friends and family have become used to my distracted comments about a poet who has been dead for nearly a century and his single-mother wife. They have their opinions too.

In Manly, after Anna and I tracked the cliff where Henry fell (or jumped), we visited Anna's mother, who lives in the beachside suburb.

'Kerrie is writing a book,' Anna told her mother.

'What about?' she replied, in her theatrical voice.

'Henry Lawson,' I said, 'the poet. He lived in Manly at one point.'

'Oh yes,' she said. 'I know his work. Why him?'

I explained about modelling in the gaol chapel that Henry wrote about; about Bertha, and the connection I felt to the story.

'Why did he go to gaol?' she asked.

'Didn't pay his child support.'

'Was he an arsehole?'

'He was a poet and an alcoholic.'

She sighed. 'He sounds like hard work. All poets are.'

Bertha never repeated the allegations of cruelty publicly, nor forced them to court. In her memoir she spoke only of his drunkenness. There's a tolerance around him that fits with the acceptance of the troubled artist. But Henry also fits too easily with today's statistics on violence at home, which show that 74 per cent of partner physical assaults involve alcohol. Norman Lindsay drew him in a rage, his cane poised over the head of a *Bulletin* colleague.[4] And Robertson warned Bertha before their wedding that Henry was a 'temperamental genius' and had 'a nasty temper'. Back then, Bertha had been idealistic, insisting 'love will keep him straight'. Idealism fades when you have your furniture repossessed and children who need food and clothing.

'Dad was quiet and he could be very gentle,' Barta recalled. In her experience, she insisted that 'when he had a drink, he would be gentler still. Of the clouded, stormy regions of my father's life, I had no personal experience. I lived remote and I knew only his affection and thoughtfulness for me.'[5]

Bertha never intimated that Henry ever hurt the children physically, although she remembered a different Henry who was drunk. She told him in her letter that she protected the children, and 'they have nearly forgotten the home scenes when you were drinking – and I will not let them see you drinking again. I train them to have the same love for you as they have for me.'[6]

But the words flung at her in biographies are relentless. Of Henry's gaoling, despite acknowledging briefly there were allegations of violence, Colin Roderick writes that 'his attitude to Bertha had turned her love to hatred'[7] and:

> Bertha saw his compositions appearing in the *Bulletin*, the *Lone Hand* and the *Worker*. She saw Lawson taking his ease at Charlemount, the Mental Hospital, the Thomas Walker Convalescent Hospital and in March with Mrs Byers ... Her resentment rose as she saw herself growing old feeding, clothing and educating the children. Once more she spun the wheels of retribution ...[8]

He theorises that Henry drank to self-medicate his undiagnosed bipolar disorder – which brought on both his creative surges and his deep depressions – and that Bertha's behaviour, and gaoling him, together curtailed his literary career and further damaged his delicate mental health.

He adds that Mary Gilmore said, 'jealousy paid a part in Bertha's remedy'.[9] Henry's assets were his portfolio of *Bulletin* articles and books. He was a celebrity writer – but he was remunerated in critical acclaim more than money. So how can you pay when you have nothing to pay with? This is what his supporters claimed, in their argument against the gaoling.

In her edited book of Louisa Lawson's *Dawn* articles, Olive Lawson wrote a footnote to 'The Divorce Extension Bill – The Drunkard's Wife':

Louisa's role in supporting the above legislation carried with it a terrible irony. A few years later these very provisions, made law in New South Wales, set in train a series of events which were to devastate Henry Lawson's life. In the early 1900s, separated from his wife and two small children, without money or property, and living on the most meagre earnings from his writing, he was unable to pay maintenance for the support of his children, and was imprisoned. This was the beginning of the most tragic pattern of events in the history of Australian literature.[10]

Bertha knew how it would be played. She told Henry in a 1903 letter, 'A man gets every one's sympathy.'[11] We can understand the complexity of it. That Bertha was a 24/7 mother, as well as earning money, seems to be ignored.

The symbols on the former morgue that's also at the National Art School are traditional Gothic symbols of mortality: the hourglass, the reverse flame, and the skull and crossbones that stalked the condemned prisoners in adjoining cells. Imagine it: shadowed by the morgue, with the sulphur-tainted air drifting through the windows, Henry pacing with 'hypnotised feet' and cursing a 'mad woman's' lies, as the gas lamps in the exercise yard flared below.

From Darlinghurst Gaol, 8 December 1909:

Dear Mrs Byers,
    ... Stevens thought I was in for £29 ... also that the order worked 'automatically' (Mrs L's word) and I 'was here whether

she liked it or no'. But I've no patience to write more, except he didn't know I was in, and out a fortnight, and in again. If the worst comes tell friends it's £15 12s., £15 12s., £15 12s. – FIFTEEN POUNDS TWELVE!!! I could shriek it out. But I'm all in the dark as to what is going on outside and perhaps I had better write no more ...

Kind remembrances to all,

Yours very truly,
Henry Lawson[12]

Mrs Byers rallied his friends, writing letters to actor and producer Bland Holt and calling on George Robertson, on behalf of Henry. She brought Henry's dinners, cradled on the long journey across the harbour from North Sydney to Darlinghurst Gaol. Outside the prison bars she was distressed.

'She was older than him, wasn't she?' Deborah Beck asks me. 'Were they lovers?'

'I don't think so. But I think she was in love with him.'

By 1905, Henry had been living with Mrs Byers for two years at various residences around the North Shore of Sydney. If they weren't lovers, they were at the very least like mother and son. Henry complained about her menagerie of cats, but he would bring home stray dogs and kittens. Mrs Byers would forgetfully leave eggs on his bed, which he – just as vague – would accidentally sit on, spreading yolk over his pants. But Henry called her affectionately the 'little woman'.

The letters to Mrs Byers are a stream of screams and pleas.

Mrs Byers told her biographer:

I feel now that what I'm going to tell will be unbelievable. The persecution he underwent was terrible and it went on for years. The cruelty of it was bad but the ignorance of his persecutors was worse. Here was a poor, underpaid writer, expected to write poetry, stories and verse as if he was a printing machine. What were his brother-writers doing? Did they fully realise the torture such a proud and sensitive man as Henry Lawson had to undergo? Did any of them busy round as I had to? Or did they let their pen-mate go to jail without a thought.

Certainly Lawson would always dip his hand in his pocket for a fellow writer when it was a much smaller question than that of jail. Yet none of them seemed to make a move to help him. Were they really indifferent or what was it? I do not blame them all though as a body, they seemed to lack the spirit of camaraderie and good fellowship.[13]

Imagine her with a warmed plate on her lap, catching the ferry to the city and then walking to Darlinghurst. Her kindness was harbour-deep. In her recollections she wrote, 'On one occasion that Henry was in jail the flesh was starved off his bones. It really looked as if his bones would rattle. This is perfectly true.'[14]

Having raised the money, Mrs Byers arranged his release: 'They called his "crime" the disobeying of an order of the court, but as he was not allowed to write in jail, so how was he to earn money? He had been put on ration No. 1 or in plain Australian, "starved" ...'[15]

Mrs Byers confided to her biographer that she was taunted by friends for her foolishness in sticking to such a 'ne'er-do-well' as Lawson; they advised her that 'he will never mend'. But she replied to them by quoting Henry's 1909 poem 'Her Vagabond Friend':

Who knows what Dame Fortune may turn in the end,
And smile, at the last, on that 'vagabond friend'.[16]

Henry's sign-off to Mrs Byers comes to mind: *Yours in trouble.*

21

Dated 2 January 1910:

Dear Harry,

I told Jim last night that you were going to take him out one day and the poor little fellow nearly cried with delight so we must not disappoint him.

Bertha came into my room and said, 'Doesn't my daddy want to see me?' I said yes, of course he did, Bertha cried, 'Take Jim out as he was sick and a day in town would do him good.'

Could I leave the children with you on Sunday afternoon for an hour or two, I have a very dear friend in St Vincent's Hospital and I want to see her on Sunday. I thought if I left the children with you, I could call later for them.

Will this arrangement suit you and then one day next week, when Jim comes to town for Physical Culture he could meet you and you could have tea together and he could come here at 5.30 and come home with me. I am so glad for his sake that you will keep – it will mean a great deal to the Boy,

I am sorry about your headache. I think it's your nerves that cause the trouble and this *[?]* plays the mischief with nervous people …

Let me know if the Sunday arrangement will suit you. If not I'll arrange for you to see the children on Saturday afternoon.

With kind wishes
I remain
Yours etc.
Bertha[1]

Henry keeps returning to conversations. Passing the former office of *The Bulletin* in the city, I say, 'Henry would hang out there and ask the *Bulletin* staff for money.'

'Poor Henry,' my friend sighs.

'Poor Henry? What about his wife and kids?'

'He was an alcoholic,' he reminds me. 'And he was a genius. He shouldn't have neglected his responsibilities to his children, but he shouldn't have gone to gaol.'

Did George Robertson have a similar thought about Henry? When the Angus & Robertson Gallery opened in 1909, Robertson installed Bertha as manager, giving her the income that Henry couldn't provide, and so building a financial buffer between Bertha and the declining writer. Henry complained to Bland Holt in a letter from gaol, written 31 October: 'And Mrs Lawson is getting good money at A & R's.'[2] So Bertha must have moved into the A & R fold in late 1909.

Henry's friends began waving the white flags: Mrs Byers' anxious and constant letters at last made his friends send around the hat.

With enough money they could send Henry to writer EJ 'Ted' Brady's bush camp, to dry out and recover from the gaoling.

Perhaps exhausted herself by the vicious cycle of summonses, gaolings and releases, Bertha was listening – despite Henry's claim that she'd told his friends that the gaoling was automatic, 'whether she liked it or no', her tone changed with the New Year. If 1909 had been characterised by hostile gaoling and pleas, she seemed to have made a New Year's resolution to try to create harmony and to emphasise the children.

And Henry wrote to Mrs Byers hopefully on 19 December 1909: 'They can't very well leave me here over Christmas; I shall probably be out on the last day (Christmas Eve).' He asked her to arrange Christmas presents for his children, and 'we'll give them a pleasant surprise on Christmas morning'.[3]

Bertha's letter of 2 January 1910 was conciliatory. She seemed to think that Henry was out of gaol once more, as he expected. But a letter from Henry sent to Mrs Byers on 5 January was addressed from the gaol's hospital, signalling he was still behind bars, albeit in medical care. He was well enough to fume: '*I authorized no one to go to Mrs Lawson* (to whom I have not spoken nor written for years) nor to attempt to make terms with her.'[4]

Bertram Stevens stepped in once more, as he had when the couple first separated, to negotiate a truce on behalf of those who had sent round the hat and formed the 'Lawson's Committee' to pay for Henry's outstanding maintenance and a trip bush. Stevens later recalled in his memoir:

> I saw Mrs Lawson & she agreed to forgo the amount [that was due to her] if we guaranteed that Lawson would leave Sydney and not molest her as he had done. We raised about 30 pounds

& I saw Lawson and offered him three alternatives – a trip around the Pacific, a visit to a station, or a visit to E.J. Brady at Mallacoota. He refused them all at first, but eventually agreed to go to Brady's place.

I might mention that as a reward for my trouble Lawson walked into my room at Allen's & without warning, struck me with his stick on the leg. I was infuriated at this & grabbed him by the collar, kicked him vigorously & ran him out.[5]

Imagine Henry brooding over his beer. He seemed to think his friends were conspiring with Bertha. In February 1910, he complained to another supporter, academic John Le Gay Brereton, who was secretary of the Lawson's Committee.

Mrs Byers was strong in her Scottish way, but by this time she was exhausted too. She wanted this to end. She wanted him home writing. She wanted to see him worried only about a starving stray he had picked up on the suburban street.

When he was released once more, she recalled how shocked she was at the state of him:

When Lawson got out of gaol his bones almost rattled. This is no exaggeration. He was a skeleton. I am not one who is inclined ordinarily to show great emotion but this time I cried when I saw him … Yet there are people who take such a thing callously, and that starving a poet is nothing. Yet this was done in a grand young country like Australia …

Yes, this was done to Henry Lawson, the most childlike and kindest heart that ever breathed … I have seen Henry Lawson bring a starved kitten or a dog in and feed it many a time. But no one seems prepared to raise a hand on his behalf. If the men of today were prepared to stop such ill treatment as this, we would say they have something to fight for. The men of today will have to answer coming generations for this treatment. As Lawson says, 'I will strike back from the grave'.[6]

22

Handwritten at Angus & Robertson Gallery, 29 January 1910:

Dear Harry,

... I can speak to you now because you are yourself. And I sincerely congratulate you and hope that you will continue and win back your health and self-respect. Before Xmas as you know things were very black with me, and I almost lost my Position.

You see no business firm will stand the private worries of an employee interfering with the Business of the day. And when you came into the gallery in the state you were in I could not do my work and the Firm strongly objected to it. How you consider that you were badly treated by me on account of the extreme steps I was forced to take with you.

But don't forget your children, and I had to take steps to protect them, if I lost my position don't you see the children could have had to go hungry at Xmas time? ...

Now I have some bad news for you ... As you know Jim has been very delicate ever since he had pneumonia in Manly about six years ago. It left the child with a cavity in the lung, and it only has been ceaseless care that has kept the boy alive ... I've spent every penny on the child's health and have been to several doctors and a month ago a consultant 'specialist' Sydney's leading doctor for children's complaints and this is what he told me. That Jim was in a very bad state indeed and that unless he had proper care it would be impossible to save him and it would be a great battle to save him ...

He ordered him to be placed under a scientific physical culture expert and Jim is now in his hands. I have to pay 4£4 quarterly fees for this alone. Jim's expenses come to 1£ weekly, or about 19/7. The child has to drink a quart of milk daily and have plenty of eggs etc, cod liver oil and other nourishment. Already there is a great improvement in the Boy and I sincerely hope it will mean renewing strength for him.

If you will help me to save Jim it will be a great comfort to you as well as to me. The child is already asking for you and begging me to take him to you. Will you see him. There is no need for you to see me at all. If you will write and say when you will see him I could make arrangements. Why not take him out one day and leave him at the door of the shop. He could come to me in the afternoon and go home with me. You could take him to Dinner in town he'd just be delighted with it.

If I did not think you were going to keep yourself I would not ask you to do this. As the sorrow of you falling back would only [?] more misery to the little fellow. The child dearly loves you and gave a boy a thrashing at school because the boy spoke slightingly of you to Jim. I never knew anything of this until a few days ago. It seems so cruel that you should not see the child now that you are yourself.

Bertha is a lovely, bright and healthy girl and will never have to face what Jim has had to do.

Re yourself. No one is more pleased to see you <u>yourself</u> again than I am. Not from any personal feelings at all. Because we both realise our Position and both know that the only bond existing between us is the children.

As far as I'm concerned, you are free as if we had never met – but that does not make me any less pleased to see you regain your manhood …

Harry do not allow a lot of foolish [?] to upset your splendid fight to regain your self respect – Don't let an idea that you are being shoved out of Sydney or that you are being influenced by your friends or indirectly by me. If so you are quite wrong …

If I were your sister I should beg of you for your own sake to leave Sydney for a little while to recover your health and strength and when you return settle down to some <u>real good work</u>.

Re the Court. If you will pay into Court whatever you <u>can afford to help with Jim</u> that will do …

I want you to help with the boy because I can never get a day beyond the dreary drudgery and the incessant worry of making ends meet and keeping out of debt. I have to pay the housekeeper 10/ weekly and have to pay a heavy rent because we must live on the heights and I have to have a balcony for Jim to sleep on. He has to sleep out winter or summer. So you can see life has not been an easy one for some years past, and if you will come forward and help it will make the burden lighter. I've had to work for eight years incessantly without ever having a holiday sometimes until eleven o'clock at night. I worked for three months from 8 o'clock until ten every night when the firm I represented was going under. So if you help me at the end of this year I may be able to take the children and I for a month's holiday.

I ask you again not to treat your real friends unkindly and above all do not let other people influence and interfere but your friends who really have your welfare at heart. When will you see Jim?

I remain yours etc,
Bertha Lawson.

PS I want you to quite understand that there is no personal reason for me writing ... as far as any personal feeling is concerned I might as well be dead. So don't be afraid that I am trying to influence you on my own behalf B.L.[1]

At Norman Lindsay's former home and studio at Springwood in the Blue Mountains, burnt trees fringe the National Trust property. His second wife, Rose Soady, is still everywhere – as a sculpture, in the artworks lining the walls, in photos and in the books in the gallery shop. The pool grove is deep and grassed.

By 1909 Lindsay had left his first wife, Katherine, known as Katie, who retreated to Brisbane, where her sister lived. Their son Jack Lindsay remembered his mother as a woman with a small bright parasol, unafraid of a herd of sullen cattle that lingered near fragile fences in the heat. But her encouraging smile during those early bewildered days in Brisbane changed and faded. He recalled the smell of gin around her friends, and his father's drawings being given away, and the anxiety and resentment he felt as the eldest male in a fatherless house, as his mother was 'beginning to give up the ghost'.[2]

A fatherless child. A retreating mother. It sounds awfully familiar.

Ten years later, in a 1919 copy of the Melbourne *Age*, wedged between an article about policemen's pay and the enticingly headlined 'Husband Orders Wife's Arrest – Sequel in Court', there was a column with the sober title 'An Artist Divorced':

> In the Divorce Court on Friday Mr Justice Gordon granted a decree nisi … in the suit in which Kathleen [*sic*] Agatha Lindsay, formerly Parkinson, petitioned for a dissolution of marriage with Norman Lindsay, the well-known artist, on the ground of his misconduct with Rose Soadey [*sic*] … Further evidence revealed that respondent was living with Miss Soadey at Springwood.[3]

His 1928 sketch *Self Portrait with Model* shows Norman seated in an armchair concentrating on his sketchpad, while a nude lounges sensuously on the chair's arm. An image search of his works reveals a blur of breasts and curls. The model in the sketch shares Rose's strong jaw.

Three years after the separation from Katie, Norman and Rose moved into this Springwood home, where siren sculptures now rise from the lawns. Rose and Norman knew Henry through *The Bulletin*. Rose recalled Henry hanging around the turnstiles at Circular Quay with a crony, waiting for her ferry to arrive when Norman and she lived across the harbour in 1909. Norman – who disliked drunks, despite his own bohemian lifestyle – tolerated Henry only because he was a *Bulletin* colleague.

Everyone has their own story, their own personality readings. In another of Norman's memoirs, *Bohemians of the Bulletin*, he included Henry among his profiles and, surprisingly, Bertha:

Lawson idolatry of today will deplore the irreverence of attaching such a label as nuisance to him, but I can assure the idolaters that they too would have dived for cover to escape Henry when he was drunk ... Henry must have been an impossible man to live with. I knew Mrs Lawson fairly well, and liked her.[4]

What? *Liked* her? So far, the only person who admitted friendship with Bertha at this time was Rose Scott, who publicly defended Bertha in a letter to the newspaper; later, Ruth Park was a friend too. Lindsay went on:

George Robertson had put her in charge of a picture gallery which he had institutioned next door to Angus and Robertson's bookshop, and as I had works on exhibition there, I often dropped in for a chat with her. She must have been a beautiful girl, and was still a very handsome woman in maturity, and from what I observed of her personality, I am sure that whatever went wrong with the Lawson marriage was not of her begetting.[5]

I'm surprised, and suspicious. Women weren't just a pretty sketch to Lindsay. He believed infidelity was part of being 'bohemian' and recalled how he and art school founder Julian Ashton once discussed adultery, arguing: 'Damn it, Julian, a man's got to have stray love affairs if he's to get anywhere in art.'[6]

Was this loyalty or flirtation with Mrs Lawson? But there seems to be nothing intended by Lindsay except a mutual respect – and perhaps disrespect for Lawson as an alcoholic:

I can only relate what I observed of it myself ... I was holding a one-man show at the gallery, and happened to be in Mrs Lawson's small office, finishing a pen sketch which had been commissioned, when she dashed in exclaiming breathlessly, 'I can't go out there. He's only come in here to annoy me.'

I glanced out, to discover that 'he' was Henry Lawson, who was going round making a pretence of looking at the pictures, in which, I am sure, he had no interest whatever, for he kept half an eye on Mrs Lawson's office door, from which she refused to emerge till he had gone. But her emotional agitation, and the intonation of that exclamation of hers, left no doubt in my mind that Henry's intrusion in the gallery was malicious.[7]

But soon Bertha was sensing a window, while Henry was sober: 'we both realise our Position and both know that the only bond existing between us is the children.'[8]

When Ruby was born she hunted for my breast while her father watched on beside me on the hospital bed. From that moment on, Dan and I were bonded together, even when we made our lives apart.

23

Sent February 1910 to Bertha Lawson at her address, Cammeray Point, North Sydney:

To Mrs Henry Lawson,

I am willing to pay so much a week into court (starting from next week) until arrears are cleared up. I would be glad to hear early what terms you suggest, trusting that you will suggest something in reason as I am pretty hard up. I would like you to know that I never asked Stevens, Ryan or anyone else to go to make terms. I have not touched a penny of the fund, nor do I intend doing so.

Yours sincerely,
Henry Lawson[1]

Back at the former gaol, outside the looming green gates, Deborah Reck points across the street at another sandstone building, next to the medical suites and apartments that carry a sign explaining Henry was a patient there, along with a plaque that reproduces his poem 'After All'.

'That was the Reception House. It was also called the Mental Hospital. He spent more time there' – she nods across the street – 'than here at the gaol. They had a room set aside for him. They called it "The Lawson Room". Sister MacCallum took him under her wing. And Mrs Byers, of course. He was looked after by women; a lot of people cared for him. He was a difficult man. They'd give him money to get out of gaol, support him, pay his rent …'

'I think Bertha was frustrated too,' I suggest.

'I think anyone who keeps destroying their life is frustrating,' she replies. 'Everyone knows people like that.'

A self-destructive Henry reluctantly went to Mallacoota with Tom Mutch and EJ Brady to recover from the gaol ordeal and, hopefully, to ignite sobriety. But he was bitter about his treatment by the courts, telling Mrs Byers 'they would crucify Christ if he came back'.[2] Maintaining the truce, however, Bertha urged him to stay around sober friends; she supported the enforced beer drought in the bush.

Henry wrote to his son, Jim, from his rural rest:

I only got your letter yesterday, and it was written nearly a month ago. We are away out of the world here, and it will take this letter a week or more to reach you. I've just come back from a 4 days' tramp up the coast and over the sandhills past Cape Howe and the cairn (a pile of stones) on the border between New South Wales and Victoria. The country is very wild and rough and there is no one there …

He added a postscript: 'I'll sell some work in Sydney, tell your mother.'[3]

At the gallery, with George Robertson's support in providing for their children, Bertha seemed more secure; she seemed hopeful that Henry would remain 'himself'. Her letters developed a cautious friendliness; she showed continuing concern for Jim's chronic lung health and shared Barta's poetry with him, though she also discussed her continually perilous finances, as she tried to balance the needs of the children. And she encouraged again, 'for the sake of the kiddies, be yourself'.[4]

In the second decade of their separation, the frustration, the hostility, the gaoling, the screaming, the pleading and the letters of demand were gradually replaced by civilised discussion of the children. Then, as the children grew older, their own voices replaced their mother's, who dropped back except for the occasional note asking politely for money and mentioning the children's successes.

The children began to write letters to their dad: at first sweet, loving and childish anecdotes about school, requests for books, art lessons, and presents sent for birthdays. Jim wrote about how his school went camping and how he was learning to swim in the surf, adding in another letter that he was going to 'Grammar school soon. Mother has had to work very hard to send me there.'[5] When she was 12, Barta herself sent Henry a poem for the first time, and then wrote thanking him for money sent for learning painting with an artist, and said that they had a little canary. She added, 'We are all very well but Mother is tired.'[6] Barta chattered about her homework and needing books. In the letter, she thanked her father for giving her money for the art lessons 'as without it Mother could not afford to have me learn what I most wish to'.[7]

Henry was responsive, and warm in his letters back to his children. There was love there. But as the children became teenagers, the letters from them to Henry were more formal and brisk. Just as he predicted and feared, they became distant emotionally as well as physically; they retreated with embarrassment from their dad when he returned to Sydney and began drinking again. Barta wrote:

> We must have seen him in the hospital in Darlinghurst because I recall being there, and Jim going off with Sister MacCallum for a holiday at Yass, and coming back with a broken arm. And I remember one long, sunny quiet day Jim and I spent with him at Walker hospital. Dad showed us all over the place, and we sat in the grounds and wandered about by the water, and in the later afternoon he saw us to the tram.
>
> As time went on, I saw less and less of him. But Jim would always find him.[8]

'Do you have children?' asks a taxi driver.

'A daughter,' I say.

'Does she look like you?'

'That's what people say,' I reply.

'It is a saying in my country, whoever the child looks like loves them the most. I have four children.'

'Do they look like you?' I ask.

'Two like me, two like her,' he says. 'So we both love. But no more.'

'No more children?' I ask, confused.

'No more wife.' He is animated at the wheel now. He gestures and sighs.

'We marry for 38 years, then enough. The way she talked to me, disgusting. So we divorce. We try again, I ask her to come back, but only if she talks to me with respect. We remarry. I say, talk to me, like I talk to you.' He speeds into a tunnel. 'But it doesn't last. We only stay together again a year and a half. Her mind is like a stone!

'But now ...' He clutches the wheel. 'I see things she likes and I buy to give to her. Then I think, why should I? Why do I? But I still do. I want to hate her, but I can't. I want to find another woman, but I still prefer her. I ask our son to ask her if she wants to come back. But he said, no she doesn't and you are better living apart – you fight.'

'So you love her, but you can't live together?' I venture.

'Yes. Maybe if I find another woman, I can forget about her.'

He brakes the cab, still talking about his ex. At the kerb I pay the fare and he drives back into his life.

24

Letter from New Zealand politician Edward Tregear, visiting Melbourne, to Bertha Lawson in Sydney. Dated Tuesday 30 May 1911, at Scott's Hotel.

My dear Bertha

I haven't yet received any note from you, so I send this to let you know that my sweet self has not yet dissolved in the sleet and wet of shivering Melbourne. I had a good night's rest in a very comfortable sleeper but next morning! Heavens! It _was_ cold. The Prime Minister of the Commonwealth happened to be at the station. There was also a deputation from the Trade Council, a poor drenched deputation. I know I shouldn't like Melbourne – great wide wet streets and huge cold palaces and such awful prices. 3/6 for each meal and 3/6 for each bed, – all the big hotels and I must stop at one because of my swell callers, the State Prime Minister, the president of the Arbitration court (Judge Higgins), the Postmaster General etc. I wish they would leave me to the poor ones.

I am to speak to 2000 people in the theatre next Sunday & I feel nervous already. But the *[?]*, the sooner I will be back to beautiful, joyous, loving-hearted Sydney. And the sweetest of all them are at 140 – N. Syd. Please give my Bertha girlie a dozen kisses from me and give Jim a good hearty pat also – I think of those dear kiddies very much. And I don't leave their kind, affectionate little mother out either, brave little woman, tender hearted little woman. Pray for the soul of a hard rider.

Yours very faithfully,
Edward Tregear[1]

Bertha never returned to court requesting a decree absolute, which would have allowed her to remarry. Henry, in a letter written soon after the judicial separation, told a friend in Hobart that he might be visiting Tasmania with a lover, explaining she was married and 'the wife won't divorce me'.[2] Although he and Bertha were divorced in all but name, Bertha clung to the 'Mrs' title and the judicial separation, in that strange borderland.

In the archives, there are some curiously tender letters to Bertha from Edward Tregear, who had helped the Lawsons secure the teaching positions in Kaikoura when they went to New Zealand.

Tregear is another man with a moustache. He's a 'soldier, surveyor, linguist, Polynesian scholar, writer, public servant, political reformer'. He 'painted landscapes (badly)'.[3] He had a poetic mindset, which you can see reflected in his letters. He married his wife, Bessie, after she divorced her first husband. So you can see too his empathy for Bertha's separation from Henry. It's intriguing whether there was any romance when he visited Australia – according to his letters, he spent the day in Manly with Bertha and the children. Their relationship may have been platonic love. Perhaps, like Henry with Mrs Byers, Bertha too wanted someone to look after her. Certainly his letters are both intimate and reassuring.

Wellington's Alexander Turnbull Library holds archives relating to Tregear, but there's no mention of Bertha Lawson in the indexes. However, she must have confided to him in her letters: writing to her on 15 September 1911 from Wellington, he called Bertha a 'plucky little soul' and said, 'I am very sorry that I find (in your last) signs both you being lonely and physically very tired. I do not know what to say except, "Cheer Up" – and that is easy to say, and hard to do.'[4]

The following year he declared to Bertha, 'I love you dearly', and called her 'Madame Brown eyes'. He had been to her home, it seems: 'I kiss your hands adieu and I shall have to withdraw my presence from the room with the creaky sofa.' He wrote to Barta too, telling her to give Jim a friendly punch and 'love to the brave tired little mother'.[5]

Reading Edward Tregear's letters, bunched in Bertha's file at the State Library of NSW, I'm reminded of my first relationship after Dan and I split up – with a French travel writer, who wrote me romantic emails every week. Still, I'm not convinced that there was a relationship between Bertha and Edward beyond a flirty friendship – perhaps, like me, she was juggling work and parenting, and corresponding with a distant lover was all she was capable of at the time.

Dan emails me from the States, which in recent months has become his new base: 'I'm getting married. I need you to send the divorce papers. I'm not getting any younger and I'm in love. We are divorced, aren't we?'

Closure was supposed to be the divorce court date, but apparently not. It takes intangible forms. I realise that he's probably never seen the certificate, issued five years before his new engagement. He was out of the country on the day, and I forwarded his certificate copy to his sister. He's never mentioned it until now.

It strikes me that the closest we've ever come to discussing our divorce is so he can marry again. The irony makes me smile.

'Why don't you have another child?' a friend asks me over drinks. 'You are still young.'

'I can't go through it alone again,' I say.

A friend of mine, who split with her partner when her son was a toddler, later re-partnered when her son was 15, and she had two babies within three years. Another friend, also a single parent, did the same when her first child was ten. People form new families.

A year after Ruby and I live with my partner, I end the relationship. We still seem to seek the pure relationship; the romance of first, second – third? – soul mates. The person who really is our destiny rather than our divorce. A relationship counsellor theorises we all live too long now for a life partner.

'We are serial monogamists,' she says. 'We used to marry as teenagers – he'd go to war or die from a disease, and she'd die in childbirth or soon after from disease too. We weren't meant to spend decades with the one person. People change too much.'

Another theory: British sociologist Catherine Hakim suggests that women have finite erotic capital, which they should exploit.

She defines erotic capital as a 'combination of beauty, social skills, good dress sense, physical fitness, liveliness, sex appeal and sexual competence'.[6] How does erotic capital hold up after one marriage, one child, and years of single parenting in conflict with relationships?

On an afternoon train, an elderly man reaches out to catch his wife shuffling on a cane as she falls down the carriage stairs. Shaking, she gains the security of her seat. He sits beside her, patting her knees while her tears roll down till the next station.

Erotic capital is only skin deep.

Later in life, when her erotic capital was supposed to be on the wane, Bertha re-partnered discreetly. A letter from Alice, Bertha's much younger sister, confided to Barta that her mother was 'all gooey' about Will Lawson and made herself 'look pretty' for her boarder.[7]

Barta recalled her mother with Will: 'They were comrades and cronies. He was good company for her, as they grew old together.' He was her 'shield from loneliness'.[8]

Will was also an alcoholic when they first met; he said that Bertha 'saved me from the grog'. It's frustrating but understandable – after what she went through with Henry, as an older and wiser woman, she still went for Henry mark II. Do we try to forge new relationships, but revert to patterns we know? Was she trying to save him because she couldn't save Henry?

Ruth Park first met Bertha and Will when 'an elderly quaint couple' came to her kitchen door to introduce themselves after the publication of her celebrated novel *The Harp in the South* in 1948. She described Will as having been 'carved from cross-grained hardwood, with a face from the British Isles' past centuries'.[9]

He introduced himself as Will Lawson and Bertha as Mrs Lawson, Park recalled. But Bertha politely corrected: 'I'm not Mrs Will Lawson, you know ... I'm Mrs Henry Lawson.'[10]

Park reflected it was 'curious the way she found Will Lawson and took him in' and that 'in Will Lawson, Bertha had achieved her simple but usually unattainable aim – she had succoured and reformed an alcoholic'. She said that Bertha had literally found Will in a gutter 15 years previously; Will told Park that at that time he was 'bust as an old paper bag' and 'sick as a dog'.[11]

'He had come to the end of his buccaneering life, his health was ruined and he had no hope,' Park wrote.

> Bertha gave him a home, fed him properly, and kept him sober. On a closed-in back verandah of Bertha's Northbridge home he had a spartan bed, a table supporting a dinosaur of a standard typewriter, files lining the walls. There he happily wrote his ballads, and books about the old whaling days in which he had a special interest. He was a man completed.
>
> Their contentment with their mutually supportive life was pleasant to see. A memory that always makes me smile is this. One morning I called unexpectedly, and found Bertha sitting on the verandah and Will absorbedly curling her hair with a wooden clothes-peg.[12]

Bertha's relationships with Henry and Will formed a triangle in her life, which she hinted at when she acknowledged Will as co-writing her memoir, *My Henry Lawson*:

> I have told it to Will Lawson to set it down. I asked him to do this because he was a member of the old ballad writers' band

and knew Harry and many of his associates; also because Harry's
stories of the courage and steadfastness of the people of the bush
inspired and encouraged Will ...[13]

Barta observed: 'If Will was a very tough bohemian, Mother had
learned to understand and enjoy Bohemia.'[14]

We are attracted to what we know.

25

Extract from an extended letter from Henry Lawson, living at Leeton, NSW, to George Robertson, dated 'January sometime, damn the date' 1917:

Dear Old George,

Your letter came as quite a refresher and at the right time ... Not that I was lonely or moody, because I've got a rush of working humour like a mountain creek that has been choked up for months and broken loose – the first time I've felt in working order for months. Besides, I'm getting my health back, feeling like my ole self – and calm. For Mrs B. has been in Sydney for nearly three weeks on holiday and I've had a rest. I needed it sorely. By a cruel irony of fate I've been having a similar time with Mrs B. to that which I had with Mrs Lawson the last year or so of our conjugal life. And by a stranger irony of fate, Mrs Lawson is writing very gentle, kindly and grateful letters. It seems strange that three of the four women I was closely connected with should develop into the Brute, so to speak. I may be meself – or because I am, and was always soft and yielding or good-natured and generous. Added to the Mater's natural bent as a selfish, indolent, mad-tempered woman, she was insanely jealous on account of my 'literary success'. Mrs L. was, of course, an insane Prussianized German, by birth on both sides, by breeding, and by nature. Mrs B. seems to have been developing into a combination of the two; and the horror of it was that there was no get-away from her here – unless I went to Narrandera (an ungodly town just outside the Area) and got drunk ...

Mrs B's pet insanity is dogs, cats, and fowls. I don't mind the fowls. But I've known her to have a clutch of chickens come out, her favourite cat eat them one after another, and then she set another hen – the tragedy to be repeated. The dog she brought up here is a fowl-killer and a man-killer – a horse-and-sulky chaser, and, all together, a dangerous dog. At least he *was*, but he isn't now. I lost him with the aid of two mates and a two-gallon jar of beer from Narrandera. She'll go raving round about it, just like Mrs L., or worse, when she comes back. You don't know what disadvantages we Australian writers labour under ...

I also lost one of Mrs B's four cats ... I don't know what's come over the poor little lady, but she seems to be developing into a regular Harpy with the tongue of a hell-hag out of Hell, and always raving about food for the animals and after money she knows I haven't got ... I've written a red-hot letter telling her I'm full up of the third instalment of my Woman-Hell-Made-Life ...

[H.L.]¹

203

Here are the 'instalments' of women in Henry's 'Woman-Hell-Made-Life': the first was his 'selfish, jealous, indolent, mad-tempered' *Mater* – Louisa, who in 1920, three years after Henry wrote this letter, passed away in Gladesville's Hospital for the Insane, Sydney, after such achievements as a suffragette and publisher.

Mrs L, the 'insane Prussianized German', was the second instalment; by then she was in the background somewhere, getting on with her life and, to his surprise, writing him 'very gentle, kindly and grateful letters'. Barta said that her mother later moved into a child-welfare career, which would have put her in contact with single parents. She was certainly interested in Henry's welfare: Mrs Byers recounted meeting Bertha during a visit to one of Henry's hospitalisations, which were becoming more frequent.

In another long and meandering letter to Robertson, discussing his autobiographical poem 'Black Bonnet', Henry reflected bitterly again on Bertha lacking her mother's sense of humour:

> Strange to say (or is it strange?) my son Jim – 6 foot 2 and twenty – has, or had, the same affection for and faith in his grandmother I had for and in mine. I must tell you about Mudder-in-Law some other time. She's got a sense of humour anyhow – can laugh even at herself as socialist and woman league-er. Had Mrs L. possessed the slightest sense of humour, things might have been very different between us, in spite of all the rest. But it is years too late for a reconciliation between us now – even if such a thing were barely possible.[2]

The third and current instalment, in his Leeton litany of complaint to George Robertson, was Mrs B, who had become a 'regular Harpy'. The kindly housekeeper was ageing and feeling the strain of now supporting Henry in Leeton, where he was supposed to be writing articles to encourage people to move into the Murrumbidgee Irrigation Area. He preferred, it seems, to be at the nearest pub.

And the fourth woman he was 'closely connected with'? Ruth Park in her memoir said she'd read Henry's letter to George Robertson, and she'd wondered if the fourth woman was his younger sister – Gertrude's twin, Annette, who had died soon after birth. But the fourth woman could be Hannah Thornburn, who, like the perfect muse, died before she could turn into a 'hell hag' like Louisa, Bertha and Mrs Byers. If Ruth Park knew about Hannah, she was too respectful of Bertha to mention her; instead, she dwelt on the rumours around Mary Gilmore, who could be another unspoken instalment, such was her self-proclaimed influence on Henry's life.

Park concluded, 'It was impossible to discern what indeed Henry Lawson wanted from women; it does not seem to have occurred to him that they wanted, needed or indeed deserved anything from him.'[3]

She recalled too, as a much younger married woman, talking to Bertha about men and, in particular, her husband D'Arcy's penchant for 'walkabouts'. Ruth says Bertha called men's immaturity hormonal: 'In some persons adolescence goes on for a very long time,' she told Ruth. 'Few adolescents know there are other people in the world. Perhaps your man is a late bloomer ... Some never do, of course.' Listening to her friend, Ruth reflected: 'I thought I detected a sigh.'[4]

To the Woman's Page, *The Bulletin*, accompanied by two portraits. No address, but thought to be 1922:

Dear Woman's Page,

I got these portraits soiled and knocked about carrying them about the country with me. When my daughter attained her degree and majority last year, as you noted in your page, you could get no late portrait of her. While in hospital, I got her to have one taken for her disreputable old dad, who has so far got over his disgust at having a Bachelor of Arts in the family, as to persuade his old heart that he'd like to see this picture in the Woman's Page.

The other portrait is of 'Jim' …

Yours,

Henry Lawson

Please return portraits – H.L.[5]

There was, of course, another woman in Henry's life, a sixth 'instalment' – his daughter, Barta. She wrote:

He tried hard to attend to my needs and he was proud of me for graduating. But always his comrade was Jim.

I remember when I had started in the library, meeting him one night in Grandma's shop and he began to ask me about my life now I had set out to work. Deeply conditioned as I always was in what to say and how to act towards him, I turned the subject lightly off with something that could draw both our attention in the shop at the moment and did not go back to it. Dad said nothing. But when I went to work I found a note from him. Such a quiet note, and oh! So deeply hurt. He said, of course he loved me, and of course he knew what his children were doing, 'but never have the slightest fear that I would come to you or give you the faintest cause for embarrassment or worry'. He never would. He never did. In all the times I saw him I had nothing from him but gentleness and love.[6]

Barta became a librarian and met writer and editor Walter Jago in 1931. He was 15 years older than she was, and had had a difficult marriage breakdown, which Barta alluded to in many of her letters to her mother that are now in the Mitchell Library. Bertha deeply disapproved of this prior separation; still, perhaps Barta understood all too well what Walter was going through, because of her own childhood, and her bitter parents.

In 1931 Barta and John Le Gay Brereton, Henry's old friend, were together editing the anthology *Henry Lawson by His Mates*, including her mother's contribution, 'Memories'. In adulthood, Barta came to see the truth about her parents' marriage:

Nobody could possibly blame Mother for separating. There was no money. They could never be happy again. There was a dreadful situation, and we were young. And afterwards there were crises, bitter for Mother and overwhelming for Dad. But all that picture of our continuing devotion simply is not true. Mother, with great determination and ability, carved out her own successful life, a life she loved and never would have changed in any circumstances, a life of high fulfilment. Dad did not figure in our scheme of things. Only Jim, without a thought, cut through it all to stand by beside him ...[7]

Ruby is studying for her music oral presentation at school. Her long ponytail hangs down her back. She is taller than me now, restless and musical. She's a lot like her dad. She chooses jazz for her presentation, and reaches into her memories of him practising when she was a baby.

'What's a jazz standard?' she asks. Dan is away, she has messaged him, but she's anxious whether she'll get him in time before the presentation.

'It's a song that all jazz musicians know,' I say. 'You know them, probably. Do you remember "Summertime"? You said that song—'

She cuts me off, laughing. 'Yes, I remember. I said it was about you and Dad.' She sings the lyric about the rich daddy and the good-looking mama.

And as I recall the next line – *hush, little baby* – I think: Ruby was that little baby, and she did cry about us.

I worry sometimes that I will be blamed for my marriage breakdown. That somehow I could have stayed, and everything would have lurched on.

'Is there a fine line between love and hate?' Ruby asks me on the bus. I grab the handrail to steady myself. Being a teenager, she's now often preoccupied by love. She continues, 'It's good you and Dad talk. You don't hate him.'

'Maybe we split before we started to hate each other. I can't hate him. I don't want to be with him, but I can't hate him. I should. But I don't.'

'It would be weird for you and Dad to still be together,' Ruby says suddenly.

'Why?' I ask.

'You are both slightly insane.'

We are staying with Ruby's cousins for the weekend when I suggest to her that we move here.

'What do you think?' I ask.

She hesitates. I'm surprised. She's asked me to do this so many times before. The beach life with her cousins will suit her. They already go to the same high school together. Ruby now takes a long and circuitous bus route from our house to get to the school, or she stays overnight with them during the week.

'I don't think you should do that for me,' she says. 'I want to live with Dad.'

'Your dad? In LA?' We are sitting on the blue-and-white wicker couches, with her cousins' dog lolling at our feet.

'I want to live with him,' she repeats, determined.

'We can talk about it,' I say cautiously.

She practises wobbly cartwheels in anticipation of cheerleading at an American school.

I can't imagine a life without her, so far away from me. For the last decade, our lives have been entwined without her dad. It was hard enough letting her stay overnight with her cousins. But I do want her to know her father.

I feel sad when I read Barta's last memories of her dad. You don't need to be separated geographically to not have a relationship. Henry and his daughter were in the same city, yet they were strangers.

I start discussing the possibility of Ruby moving in with her father. His wife is enthusiastic and she envisions Ruby and a baby living in their house. Happy families. In the months that follow they often Skype, and then Ruby goes to visit them for school holidays, to meet her new stepmother.

I should be jealous, but I'm so grateful to this woman for doing what I couldn't – giving Ruby a father.

'Don't screw this up,' I tell him. It's not too late.

26

By 1917 Henry and Bertha's acrimony had faded like the calligraphy ink on their divorce papers. And in 1922, Darlinghurst Gaol began its metamorphosis from bars and brutality into the East Sydney Technical College, which later became the National Art School. Artists and models began to flow through the gates that once locked Henry from the street.

I'm given an oval, unattributed miniature of a frail man with big brown eyes, around which the artist has painted deep wrinkles and bags bulging with ill health. It might be Henry Lawson: the man in the portrait has Henry's eyes and a moustache, but the moustache seems too thin. It is frail, like the man. A photo of Henry taken in 1922, at a wharf, in a suit and hat, is different – even with the pixelation of the enlargement, his moustache is still squirrel thick.

Henry remained a face in the street that people recognised, but he was now regarded with curiosity and pity rather than admiration. Although he was still being published by *The Bulletin*, Mary Gilmore wrote that Henry was 'bitter and sad' about the disdain he felt at the *Bulletin* office 'because he was no longer on top of the wave'.[1] He hobbled there on a stick, partially paralysed after a stroke. Now 56, he was tired and frail; he shook.

Maybe the mysterious, unsigned portrait is of Henry in his final days. Shuffling from bookshop to bottle shop to the *Bulletin* office, where Mary Gilmore said 'he was treated with rudeness and contempt',[2] Henry became a caricature of the alcoholic bohemian writer. EJ 'Ted' Brady, visiting Sydney from Queensland, found him in the cashier's office at *The Bulletin*, arguing. He offered to take Henry for a drink:

> It was a yarn I wanted, more than refreshment; but I had promised his wife twenty years previously that I would not drink with him. Twenty years being, penally, the term of a man's natural life, we agreed that there could be no great breach of faith in the matter; especially as I was going no further down the broad path with him than the demon of dry ginger ale could drag me – and for other reasons. I had not seen him for some time and noticed that he had aged in appearance. He put down the tankard and took up the pipe in a tired way ... I took him by the sleeve, looked into those brown spaniel eyes – there was a light in them I had never seen there before, the homing light – and said with a heartiness I did not quite feel:
>
> 'You —— old sinner, you ought to have been dead long ago!'
>
> 'Why? Why did you think that?'
>
> 'The way you knock yourself about.'
>
> He pretended to think it over very carefully – a way he had.
>
> 'Beer saved my life,' he said at last in a voice of simple conviction.
>
> 'Beer?'

'Yeth, Ted – *Beer*'

'I cannot see how beer preserved your life.'

'Well,' he clinched, after taking a long pull, 'it *did*. If I'd been drinking hard tack I *would* have been dead long ago.'[3]

On the night of 1 September 1922, Henry was at the Abbotsford cottage in which he lived with Mrs Byers. After the evening meal and ale, he told Mrs Byers he'd rest, then write all night. She kept the kettle on, as it was normal for him to have tea later.

Around 9 pm, when she was in bed, she heard a cry: 'Little woman!'

Later she wrote: 'Now I sadly sit and ponder and his voice seems ever near saying, "Come, bring your chair on this side, sit close that I may hear." Ah me, it cuts me like a knife, the things that once have been.'[4]

27

Dated 8 September 1922 to Dame Mary Gilmore, care of *The Worker* Office, St Andrews Place:

Madam,

Your letter to the Daily Mail was shown to me this morning. I could expect nothing else from you. Too long have I kept *silent* so that Harry's memory should never suffer. Now when I return to Sydney I shall let the public know the truth both as to yourself, and as to Mrs Byers. You are *not* aware that the Captain of the ship (the Karlsruhe) gave me your letter that you had posted to my husband. That letter had been shown to the late Mr Farrell of the Daily Telegraph. Also to several other friends in Sydney who know the true facts of your conduct in my home in England and also on the voyage to Australia.

It would be impossible to appeal to any womanly feeling in you. May I ask you to refrain from rushing to pose as a friend of my late husband.

Yours etc,
Bertha Lawson.[1]

Henry's women came to the funeral. Mary Gilmore; his daughter, Barta; Mrs Byers; Bertha. All staring at his casket, adorned with wattle.

Writer Zora Cross said the women wept together. 'I heard from Mrs Jago [Barta] Mrs Byers broke down at the graveside. She told me that Mrs Byers sat apart weeping bitterly afterwards and Mrs Lawson went over to her and comforted her.'[2]

But still it went on. In the days after the funeral, Mary and Bertha clashed yet again. On 8 September, Mary's letter was published in the Sydney *Daily Mail*, paying tribute to the grieving 'little landlady' and calling for an allowance in recognition of her caring for the poet until his death.

Mrs Byers, Mary wrote,

> for so many years kept house for Lawson, figures so often in his writings, cared for him in sickness and in health, and was with him to the last. As a woman and as an Australian, I wish to pay my tribute to Mrs Byers, whose declining years begin to fall heavily upon her …
>
> I would like to suggest that either by public subscription or through the State, the house Henry Lawson died in, or one in which he had lived, be bought and 'the little landlady' installed with a sufficient allowance, or salary, as caretaker for such Lawson relics as may be kept there.

She concluded: 'It seems a thing a woman should suggest if only in recognition of another woman's long and faithful friendship with Lawson – Yours, etc., MARY GILMORE.'[3]

Initially it reads as it appears – a tribute to Mrs Byers, the little landlady. Bertha's warning letter in response, written later that day in a flare of anger, seems disproportionate to the words. But thinking about what the letter implies, the scalpel slices subtly through the text. Mary was reminding Bertha – and the public – that she judicially separated from Henry and had no part in his later life, and therefore had no right to his legacy. She implied that there was only one woman left in Henry's life who had loved him this way – Mrs Byers.

Rose Scott clarified the searing subtext when she defended Bertha later that month in a letter to *The Sydney Morning Herald*:

As one who has been on the most intimate terms of friendship with the family for a quarter of a century I have been much pained and greatly grieved at statements (not in the 'Herald') which seem to belittle and discredit his widow and children. Knowing as I do the noble part that Mrs. Bertha Lawson has played during the whole period of our friendship, knowing the bitter anguish she has suffered and the strenuous time through which she has passed while making a home and educating her two children, knowing how both for the sake of the children and their father she has suffered in silence during all those long, weary, heartbreaking years, it does seem to me the very utmost refinement of cruelty that one word should have been uttered which was calculated to give her pain.

In conclusion I would express my honest conviction that no truer or more loyal woman, no more loving, devoted, and self-sacrificing mother ever lived, toiled, and suffered for children and husband than the widow of Australia's greatest writer and sweetest songster, Henry Lawson. I am, etc., ROSE SCOTT.[4]

216

After Mary had received Bertha's warning letter responding to her tribute to Mrs Byers, and reminding her of their clashes in England and aboard the *Karlsruhe* two decades earlier, Mary, in an equal flare of ink, sat down and began her never-published memoir, 'Henry Lawson and I', in which she detailed her friendship with Henry and her enduring animosity towards Bertha. The he-said-she-said continued.

In this memoir, Mary also claimed that she knew about Henry's death before Bertha did. She received the news from Phillip Harris, the photographer who in 1922 took that last photo of Henry, on the wharf.

Harris had apparently gone to Abbotsford, where Mary said he found

> Henry dead on the floor in a corner in his room and two of Mr George Robertson's men there. Mrs Byers was stupefied by shock. He [Harris] told me of the bare scantily furnished room, of the undrawn blinds, of the poor body under a dirty blanket on the floor, and of the absence of anyone able to look after him save helpless, poor old Mrs Byers.[5]

Harris asked the NSW premier for a state funeral, but was refused. Mary suggested going higher: 'Suddenly I remembered that the Prime Minister, Mr W.M. Hughes, was to be in Sydney that evening or next morning. "Hughes" I said. "He will give a state funeral, no question about that!"' The Journalists' Association approached Billy Hughes, who granted the funeral that she claimed she and Harris organised. So she was miffed when she read comments by Barta in the *Daily Mail* that the funeral arrangements for the service at St Andrew's Cathedral had been in consultation with the family:

The remark made by Lawson's friends was: 'She is very much her mother's daughter!' No arrangements were made in consultation with them; they had not even troubled to enquire after him, alive or dead. For months he had lived where he died, and had been in the house of his last days for two or three weeks. His address was known as at Angus & Robertson ... *The Bulletin* ... to scores of others. It was always available and never secret ... Mrs Lawson did not wish to go to the funeral. Phillip Harris persuaded her saying that in after years the children might regret it if they did not appear, and also, because it would create talk if none of them were there.[6]

The Sydney Morning Herald and other Sydney papers reported Bertha was indeed there, at 'one of the simplest yet most impressive services heard in the Cathedral'. Under 'The Mourners' the *Herald* began, 'The chief mourners and relatives were:– Mrs. Henry Lawson (widow), Miss Bertha and Mr. James Lawson (children), Mrs. G. O'Connor (sister), Mr. Peter Lawson and Mr. Charles Lawson (brothers)'. It then listed other relatives and family friends, including Mrs Byers.[7]

Mary clearly thought top position should have been awarded to Mrs Byers and herself. But it was three paragraphs down, after the federal and state politicians, and university representatives, that the paper finally listed 'Mary Gilmore' buried among the names of Henry's bohemian friends.

In 1931, nine years after the funeral, Bertha attended the unveiling of Henry's statue in The Domain by Governor-General Sir Philip Game. She stood on the ceremonial platform with their children and her sister, Hilda, wife of Premier Jack Lang.

Yet neither Bertha's prominent presence nor the statue's unveiling sat well with some of Henry's friends. It was seen as a mockery of the neglect that had been shown to him in his later years. Ted Brady despaired of the literary lionising after his death: 'It makes me sick – this posthumous exaltation of a writer, who was scorned and exploited while living, and whose value was only recognized after he was well underground.'[8]

Bertha, however, seems to have welcomed the celebrations, as did Barta. Jim, who became a schoolteacher, retreated into his life, leaving a few letters and drawings that have been swept up into the archives with other memories. Barta's co-edited anthology was published to coincide with the unveiling of George Lambert's statue. As well as her contribution to that book, in 1943 Bertha published her memoirs, pointedly called *My Henry Lawson*. Two years later – by now a middle-aged lady in glasses, hat and printed dress – she unveiled the Henry Lawson Memorial College with Premier William McKell. She popped up at a memorial to Henry Lawson at Eurunderee with Clive Evatt. Streets and reserves were opened by her. She was in demand for ribbon cutting. She was loyal to the legend that now surrounds Henry.

Her critics said she'd grasped only one thing: his fame.

Mrs Byers retreated into obscurity, and into her memories. Mary Gilmore's call for a public fund for Mrs Byers was forgotten, like the woman herself. Zora Cross wrote:

> I don't know what happened to Mrs Byers. She seemed to be very poor. I heard of her once more a couple of years after Lawson's death. Mrs Lucy Cassidy, who was then Nurse Sullivan, nursed

Lawson in his last illness and she was my nurse at the time. She mentioned Mrs Byers to me. She told me that Mrs Byers was subject to fainting turns and liked smelling salts, which she couldn't afford to buy. Lucy said that Mary Gilmore had bought a rather expensive bottle of the stuff for Mrs Byers when she found she hadn't any.

Mary Gilmore had the salts inscribed: '*Presented to Mrs Byers, friend of Henry Lawson by Mary Gilmore*'. Mrs Byers thought it too grand to use and never used the bottle. She regarded it as a Lawson relic, which it was undoubtedly. I had a bottle of smelling salts, which was open and reminded me of the other. Naturally I insisted Lucy take it to Mrs Byers on the understanding it was to be used and that she didn't say who had sent it. I hope it was.[9]

Barta mourned her father, regretting her remoteness:

I was told, after his funeral, that just before he died he had a garbled message, that he thought was from me, to meet him at a City corner. I heard that, exhausted and sick as he was, he went there and stood for long over an hour and would not go away, in hope that I might come …

Someone I knew very well asked me after he died, 'Bertha, seeing your Father as we did in the last years, derelict about the City streets, tell me could you love him? Could you be proud of him, for himself, as a man?' Yes, I could be very proud of him, for himself, as a man. He had nothing but look what he gave. And look what he gave to me, love, freedom, joy in life, everything I dreamed about, everything I hoped for. It came from him. If it had not been for him Walter's [Jago] strong hands could never have lifted me out of my own loneliness and deep distress. If I had not edited the 'Mateship' book with Walter we would have never known companionship and love with all that went with it, and all that came after. Quite simply and sincerely I owe him my whole happiness. It was his gift to me. I can love him because he stands above us all. Because his fun and his friendship, his troubled, tragic spirit, his rugged ways, the vision that he never lost, the hopes that were all broken, his kindness and despair, his heart and soul poured out, everything he thought and everything he wrote for our great heritage, were as much a part of him as his drinking. And I am like him, and I understand.[10]

28

The coastal walk curls around to Waverley Cemetery. There are 50,000 gravesites spread across the cliff top. A crowd of ghosts. The sun bleaches the headstones and mottles the cement. Hardy weeds coil over the plots and grow through cracked marble tiles. The sea salt blows in, corroding memorial plates to an eerie green. The old palms are windburnt. Nothing fragile lives here except faith.

Deeper into the cemetery are crumbling statues and forgotten crypts. I get lost among the angels. A lawnmower's grinding hum breaks the quiet. A man dressed in gardening gear, to protect his ears and skin from the noise and the sun, is mowing the grassy aisles that branch off the cemetery roads. The grass is dying in the summer heat.

He stops the mower and takes off his earmuffs and sunglasses. The sunglass mark around his eyes is as white as the marble statues around us.

'Where's Henry Lawson's grave?' I ask.

'Yeah,' he says, thinking. Then he points along the road. 'Down there, and turn left. It's up there. There's a sign.' The mower grinds back to the grass.

A ute blocks the cemetery road and two maintenance men are shifting sand. Another lies on a grassy grave.

Further on, 'Henry Lawson this aisle' is handpainted on a peeling post.

I walk up the path, with graves either side. A newspaper photo taken on the day of his funeral showed hundreds of mourners gathered around his grave. All the plots look forgotten now. Mary Gilmore said that she wanted him moved to a more prominent position in the cemetery, but Bertha wouldn't allow it. A fight to the end.

Headstones are squeezed like terraces along the row. How Sydney, eternally finding any spare space with a water view. Henry would have appreciated that. His grave is raised on a bed of stone and scattered with gravel, topped with a large faded shell, two smaller conches and a dried, curled starfish.

Given he was the 'bush poet', it's surprising to see shells on Henry's grave. The quotation inscribed onto the stone reads:

> Love hangs about thy name like music round a shell
> No heart can take of thee a tame farewell.

At the bottom of the gravestone, another plaque is inscribed, 'In Loving Memory of *his wife* Bertha Marie Louise Lawson Died 19 July 1957, aged 81 years.'

Despite the court orders, the fights, the gaoling, the suffering, Bertha and Henry have been buried together. His wife is a footnote on his life.

Ruby cuts out letters spelling 'Free' and pastes them on her guitar case. Wanderer's blood.

Her cat paces around her as she packs. She is travelling with her aunt and cousin to Los Angeles and, for the first time since she was four, she will be living with her father again.

The airport shifts with people. Flight times roll over on the departure screens. Ruby's blond ponytailed cousin bounces on the food court chair.

We walk together to Customs.

I can't go any further with her.

Runners sweat on the path past Henry's statue in The Domain. Storm clouds mount behind the city skyline.

The swag is at the back of the statue. To fill pages over the languid January weeks, *The Australian* has been running extracts from the *Penguin Book of Australian Bush Writing*, and has republished Lawson's short story 'The Romance of the Swag', written in 1907, four years after Bertha filed for judicial separation.

Henry's first paragraph struck me:

> The Australian swag fashion is the easiest way in the world of carrying a load. I ought to know something about carrying loads: I've carried babies, which are the heaviest and most awkward and heartbreaking loads in this world for a boy or man to carry, I fancy. God remember mothers who slave about the housework (and do sometimes a man's work in addition in the bush) with a heavy, squalling kid on one arm![1]

No, the heaviest load is leaving the child. That's the burden. A swag of guilt is carried by the roaming, solitary father, made heavier still with the yearning felt by the child who has been left, often before they understand.

When my daughter's father began a life with a suitcase swinging by his side, he said, 'You know, the second time I went away, I saw you and Ruby standing on the steps. You both looked so sad. I nearly stopped the cab.'

I touch the sandstone blocks that raise Henry high.

He stands over me. The gum leaves are as still.

—— Acknowledgements ——

This book began as a memoir of single parenting. After I discovered the story of Bertha Lawson, it also became a work of history. I was encouraged to keep researching and writing by Megan Le Masurier and Fiona Giles, at the University of Sydney; and Richard Walsh. Thanks also to Merran White and John Hyde and their dog, Dude, for being my second home in Melbourne while I researched there.

UQP publisher Alexandra Payne and editors Judith Lukin-Amundsen and Ian See embraced this book with their advice and editing skills.

I spent many hours researching at the State Library of NSW and State Library Victoria, and at the State Archives of NSW, assisted by their wonderful librarians. Professor Colin Roderick, Professor Manning Clark, Olive Lawson, Brian Matthews, and Meg Tasker and Lucy Sussex all published invaluable texts about Henry and Louisa Lawson; and Deborah Beck illuminated the former Darlinghurst Gaol during our meeting at the National Art School.

A memoir is not just your memories. So most of all I wish to thank my family and friends who graciously contributed their stories to the book; allowed me to write about memories I share with them; and patiently listened to me wonder aloud about a long-ago poet and his single-parent wife.

I am grateful for permission to reproduce copyright material in this book: Extract from Olive Lawson (ed.), *The First Voice of Australian Feminism* copyright © Olive Lawson, reproduced with permission of the author. Extracts from Norman Lindsay's *Bohemians of the Bulletin* copyright © H. C. & A. Glad, reproduced with permission of Barbara Mobbs. Material from the Lothian Publishing Company records 1895–1950, MS 6026, State Library Victoria, reproduced with permission of State Library Victoria. Extracts from Brian Matthews' *Louisa* copyright © Brian Matthews, reproduced with permission of the author. Permission to reproduce extracts from an unpublished interview with Bertha Lawson by Ruth Park and from Ruth Park's memoir *Fishing in the Styx*, Viking Penguin Books Australia, 1993, courtesy Tim Curnow Literary Agent & Consultant, Sydney. Extracts from Colin Roderick's *Henry Lawson: A Life* and letters from *Henry Lawson Letters: 1890–1922*, copyright © Colin Roderick and HarperCollins Australia, reproduced with permission of HarperCollins Australia.

Endnotes

Prologue

1   Bertha's full name was in fact Bertha Marie Louise Lawson, but the affidavit has 'Louisa' throughout.

2   NRS 13495 Divorce case papers #4676 Bertha Lawson, 1903, State Records Authority of NSW.

3   Henry Lawson, letter to Bertha Lawson, n.d., Lawson family papers 1896–1968, MLMSS 7692 1 (1), State Library of NSW.

Chapter 1

1   Will Carter, 'Will Carter's Notes: Australianites', *The Daily Advertiser Wagga Wagga*, 14 July 1930, p. 4. https://trove.nla.gov.au/newspaper/article/142690986

2   'Lawson Memorial: Model on View', *The Sydney Morning Herald*, 26 March 1930, p. 14. http://trove.nla.gov.au/newspaper/article/16636567/1191491 Also see National Gallery of Australia, 'George W Lambert Retrospective: Heroes and Icons: Henry Lawson Memorial 1927–31', http://nga.gov.au/exhibition/lambert/Detail. cfm?IRN=163409.

3   Andrew Motion, *The Lamberts*, Farrar, Straus and Giroux, New York, 1986, p. 110.

4   'Henry Lawson: Memorial Statue Unveiled', *The Sydney Morning Herald*, 29 July 1931, p. 10. http://trove.nla.gov.au/newspaper/article/16796350

5   Denton Prout, *Henry Lawson: The Grey Dreamer*, Rigby, Sydney, 1963, p. 220.

6   'Drought Relief Concert', *The Sydney Morning Herald*, 3 April 1903, p. 6. http://trove.nla.gov.au/newspaper/article/14555383 'Women's League',

The Sydney Morning Herald, 3 April 1903, p. 6. http://trove.nla.gov.au/newspaper/article/14555345 'Attempted Wife Murder: Assailant Out Of Danger', *The Sydney Morning Herald*, 3 April 1903, p. 5. http://trove.nla.gov.au/newspaper/article/14555169/1335463

Chapter 2

1 Henry Lawson, 'After All', *The Bulletin*, 28 March 1896, p. 13. Also included in Henry Lawson, *In the Days When the World Was Wide: And Other Verses*, Angus & Robertson, Sydney, 1900, pp. 216–217.

2 Bertha Lawson, *My Henry Lawson*, Frank Johnson, Sydney, 1943.

3 Bertram Stevens, 'Henry Lawson', Angus & Robertson Publishing Manuscripts A 1889, State Library of NSW, 1917.

4 Bertha Lawson, *My Henry Lawson*, p. 33.

5 Verity Burgmann, 'McNamara, Matilda Emilie Bertha (1853–1931)', *Australian Dictionary of Biography*, National Centre of Biography, Australian National University, 1986. http://adb.anu.edu.au/biography/mcnamara-matilda-emilie-bertha-7431

6 Bertha Lawson, 'Memories', in Bertha Lawson [Jago] and J Le Gay Brereton (eds), *Henry Lawson by His Mates*, Angus & Robertson, Sydney, 1931, pp. 81–82.

7 Ruth Park, manuscript notes of interview with Bertha Lawson, 1952, Ruth Park and D'Arcy Niland literary papers 1950–1992, MLMSS 8078/Series 3/Box 12, State Library of NSW.

8 ibid.

9 Ruth Park, *Fishing in the Styx*, Penguin, Melbourne, 1993, p. 193.

10 Mary Gilmore, 'Personal History: Henry Lawson and I', c. 1922, Dame Mary Gilmore papers 1911–1954, A3292, State Library of NSW. Also in Colin Roderick, *Henry Lawson: A Life*, Angus & Robertson, Sydney, 1999, p. 147.

11 Ruth Park, *Fishing in the Styx*, p. 194.

12 Rebecca Wiley quoting George Robertson's conversations with Bertha appears in Colin Roderick, *Henry Lawson: A Life*, p. 147. Roderick cites the original source as: '"Recollections of George Robertson" in private possession' (p. 424). Bertha Lawson also recalls the conversation in *My Henry Lawson*, p. 37.

13 Louisa Lawson, 'Unhappy Love Matches', *The Dawn*, vol. 2, no. 2, 1889, in Olive Lawson (ed.), *The First Voice of Australian Feminism: Excerpts from Louisa Lawson's The Dawn 1888–1895*, Simon and Schuster, Sydney, 1990, p. 28.

14 Bertha Lawson [Jago], unpublished notes, n.d., Lawson family papers 1896–1968, MLMSS 7692 1 (1), State Library of NSW.

15 Bertha Lawson, 'Memories', pp. 84–86.

16 Bertha Lawson, *My Henry Lawson*, p. 39.

17 Aubrey C Curtis (ed.), 'Reminiscences of Henry Lawson by Isabel Byers', c. 1925,

in Lawson family papers, including papers of Isabel Byers relating to Henry Lawson, 1892–1925, MLMSS 3694/Box 2/Folder 2, State Library of NSW.

18   Ruth Park, interview with Bertha Lawson, 1952.

19   Bertha Lawson, *My Henry Lawson*, p. 39.

20   Cyril Pearl, *Wild Men of Sydney*, Lansdowne, Melbourne, 1958, pp. 11–12.

21   Norman Lindsay, 'Circular Quay in the Nineties', in *Bohemians of the Bulletin*, Angus & Robertson, Sydney, 1977, pp. 8–9.

22   Quoted in Colin Roderick, *The Real Henry Lawson*, Rigby, Adelaide, 1982, p. 45. Roderick does not reference the original source.

23   The Johnson Studios, portrait of JF Archibald and Henry Lawson, Sydney, 1918, in Ferguson collection of photographs, National Library of Australia.

24   Bertha Lawson, *My Henry Lawson*, p. 40.

25   ibid., p. 46.

26   Bertram Stevens, 'Henry Lawson'.

27   ibid.

28   Bertha Lawson, *My Henry Lawson*, p. 55.

29   Bertram Stevens, 'Henry Lawson'.

30   ibid.

Chapter 3

1   Henry Lawson, letter to Hugh Maccallum, 25 June 1897, in Colin Roderick (ed.), *Henry Lawson Letters: 1890–1922*, Angus & Robertson, Sydney, 1970, pp. 71–72.

2   Bertha Lawson, *My Henry Lawson*, p. 51.

3   Bertha Lawson, 'Memories', p. 96.

4   Ruth Park, *Fishing in the Styx*, p. 193.

5   WH Pearson, *Henry Lawson among Maoris*, Australian National University Press, Canberra, 1968, p. 83.

6   Bertha Lawson, 'Memories', pp. 95–96.

7   ibid., p. 97–99.

8   ibid., p. 83.

9   Henry Lawson, letter to the Secretary for Education, Wellington, 28 September 1897, in Colin Roderick (ed.), *Henry Lawson Letters: 1890–1922*, p. 78.

10   Bertha Lawson, 'Memories', pp. 99–100.

11   ibid., pp. 106–107.

12   Denton Prout, *Henry Lawson: The Grey Dreamer*, p. 165.

13   Henry Lawson, 'Water Them Geraniums', c. 1901, in Leonard Cronin (ed.), *A Camp-Fire Yarn: Henry Lawson Complete Works 1885–1900*, Redwood, Melbourne, 2000, p. 721.

14   Bertha Lawson [Jago], unpublished notes, n.d.

Chapter 4

1 Bertram Stevens, 'Henry Lawson'.

2 Colin Roderick, *Henry Lawson: A Life*, 1991, p. 197.

3 George A Taylor, *Those Were the Days: Being Reminiscences of Australian Artists and Writers*, Tyrell's, Sydney, 1918, pp. 10–11.

4 ibid., p. 11.

5 ibid.

6 Manning Clark, *In Search of Henry Lawson*, Macmillan, Melbourne/Sydney, 1978, pp. 82–83.

7 George A Taylor, *Those Were the Days*, p. 20.

8 ibid., p. 23.

9 Bertha Lawson, 'Memories', p. 107.

10 Norman Lindsay, *Bohemians of the Bulletin*, p. 7.

11 Henry Lawson, letter to Dr Frederick Watson, c. 1916, in. Colin Roderick (ed.), *Henry Lawson Letters 1890–1922*, p. 237.

12 Bertha Lawson, 'Memories', p. 107.

13 Denton Prout, *Henry Lawson: The Grey Dreamer*, p. 174. He cites the original source as Jack Lang, *I Remember*, c. 1956.

14 Fred Broomfield, 'Recollections of Henry Lawson', in Bertha Lawson [Jago] and J Le Gay Brereton (eds), *Henry Lawson by His Mates*, p. 66.

15 Henry Lawson, 'The Sex Problem Again', in *The Children of the Bush*, Methuen, London, 1902, pp. 127–132. Also see Leonard Cronin (ed.), *A Camp-Fire Yarn: Henry Lawson Complete Works 1885–1900*, pp. 544–545.

16 'Rest Haven: Sydney's Temperance Sanatorium for Male Inebriates: A Visitor's Impressions', *Evening News*, 6 June 1896, p. 5. http://trove.nla.gov.au/newspaper/article/108780946

17 Henry Lawson, 'The Boozers' Home', in *The Children of the Bush*, pp. 121–126. Also appears in Leonard Cronin (ed.), *A Camp-Fire Yarn: Henry Lawson Complete Works 1885–1900*, p. 616.

18 ibid.

19 Hannah's correct name is Hannah Thornburn, according to Colin Roderick, who attributes the spelling variation in the poem title 'Hannah Thomburn' to a typeset error in printing. See 'Henry Lawson and Hannah Thornburn', *Meanjin Quarterly*, vol. 27, no. 1, p. 74.

20 Henry Lawson, letter to George Robertson, received 9 February 1917, in Colin Roderick (ed.), *Henry Lawson Letters 1890–1922*, p. 271.

21 Colin Roderick, *The Real Henry Lawson*, p. 89.

22 Bertram Stevens, 'Henry Lawson'.

23 Bertha Lawson, 'Memories', p. 108.

24 Aubrey C Curtis (ed.), 'Reminiscences of Henry Lawson by Isabel Byers'.
25 Fred Broomfield, 'Recollections of Henry Lawson', p. 68.
26 ibid., p. 71.
27 ibid., p. 72.
28 Henry Lawson, 'For He Was a Jolly Good Fellow', n.d., in Leonard Cronin (ed.), *A Fantasy of Man: Henry Lawson Complete Works 1901–1922*, Lansdowne, Sydney, 1984, p. 338.
29 Henry Lawson, 'The Longstaff Portrait', n.d., in Leonard Cronin (ed.), *A Fantasy of Man: Henry Lawson Complete Works 1901–1922*, p. 926.
30 Bertha Lawson, *My Henry Lawson*, p. 72.

Chapter 5
1 Bertha Lawson, letter to Bertha McNamara, 30 July 1900, Lawson family papers 1896–1968, MLMSS 7692 1 (1), State Library of NSW.
2 Henry Lawson, letter to George Robertson, c. August 1900, in Colin Roderick (ed.), *Henry Lawson Letters 1890–1922*, p. 127.
3 Henry Lawson, letter to *The Australian Star*, April 1900, in Colin Roderick (ed.), *Henry Lawson Letters 1890–1922*, p. 126.
4 Bertha Lawson, 'Memories', p. 111.
5 ibid., pp. 113–114.
6 Bertha Lawson, *My Henry Lawson*, p. 74.

Chapter 6
1 Bertha Lawson, letter to Bertha McNamara, 18 July 1900 (but thought to be 1901), Lawson family papers 1896–1968, MLMSS 7692 1 (1), State Library of NSW.
2 Bertha Lawson, letter to Bertha McNamara, 11 September 1900, Lawson family papers 1896–1968, MLMSS 7692 1 (1), State Library of NSW.
3 Quoted in Meg Tasker and Lucy Sussex, '"That Wild Run to London": Henry and Bertha Lawson in England', *Australian Literary Studies*, vol. 23 no. 2, 2007, pp. 168–184. Original appears in AG Stephens papers 1859–1933, MLMSS 4937/20, State Library of NSW.
4 Maude Wheeler, 'The Lights of London', *Truth*, 28 April 1901, p. 8. Also referred to in Tasker and Sussex, '"That Wild Run to London"', and Colin Roderick, *Henry Lawson: A Life*, 1991.
5 Quoted in Tasker and Sussex, '"That Wild Run to London"', p. 173.
6 ibid., p. 175. Tasker and Sussex cite 'Red Page', *The Bulletin*, 24 May 1902.
7 Henry Lawson, 'Triangles of Life', *Triangles of Life and Other Stories*, Standard Publishing, Melbourne, 1913.

8   Andrew Roberts, *The Lunacy Commission: A Study of Its Origin, Emergence and Character*, section 3.8, 1981. http://studymore.org.uk/01.htm

9   Bethlem Royal Hospital, patient admission and casebooks 1683–1932, London.

10 ibid.

11 Quoted in Tasker and Sussex, '"That Wild Run to London"', p. 172.

12 Bertha Lawson, letter to Bertha McNamara, 2 November 1901, Lawson family papers 1896–1968, MLMSS 7692 1 (1), State Library of NSW.

13 Bethlem Royal Hospital Archives and Museum, 'In the Spotlight: Relatives 2', *Bethlem Blog*, 22 August 2011. https://bethlemheritage.wordpress.com/2011/08/22/in-the-spotlight-relatives-2/

14 Mary Gilmore, 'Personal History: Henry Lawson and I'.

15 Bertha Lawson, 'Memories', pp. 114–115.

16 Bertha Lawson, *My Henry Lawson*, p. 74.

Chapter 7

1   Henry Lawson, letter to David Scott Mitchell, 11 February 1902, in Colin Roderick (ed.), *Henry Lawson Letters 1890–1922*, pp. 131–132.

2   Bertha Lawson, letter to Bertha McNamara, 2 November 1901, Lawson family papers 1896–1968, MLMSS 7692 1 (1), State Library of NSW.

3   Mary Gilmore, 'Personal History: Henry Lawson and I'.

4   ibid.

5   ibid.

6   ibid.

7   ibid.

8   ibid.

9   ibid.

10 ibid.

11 ibid.

12 ibid.

13 ibid.

14 Randolph Bedford, 'Letters from Exile', *The Critic*, 10 October 1903, p. 13. http://trove.nla.gov.au/newspaper/article/211401324/23511901 Also see Lucy Sussex, 'A Gum-Tree Exile: Randolph Bedford in England and Italy', *PORTAL Journal of Multidisciplinary International Studies*, vol. 10, no. 1, 2013. https://epress.lib.uts.edu.au/journals/index.php/portal/article/view/2379

15 Mary Gilmore, 'Personal History: Henry Lawson and I'.

16 ibid.

17 'Arrival of the *Karlsruhe*', *The Sydney Morning Herald*, 21 July 1902, p. 8. http://trove.nla.gov.au/newspaper/article/14434941

18 Ruth Park, *Fishing in the Styx*, p. 193.

19 Bertha Lawson, *My Henry Lawson*, p. 79.

20 ibid.

Chapter 8

1 Henry Lawson, 'To Hannah', *The Bulletin*, 1 September 1904, p. 3.

2 Mary Gilmore, 'Personal History: Henry Lawson and I'.

3 Bertha Lawson, *My Henry Lawson*, pp. 79–80.

4 Mary Gilmore, 'Personal History: Henry Lawson and I'.

5 Quoted in Colin Roderick, 'Henry Lawson and Hannah Thornburn', p. 87.

6 ibid., p. 79.

7 Colin Roderick, *Henry Lawson: A Life*, 1991, p. 245.

8 Colin Roderick, 'Henry Lawson and Hannah Thornburn', p. 87.

Chapter 9

1 Bertha Lawson, letter to Henry Lawson, c. 1902, in Lothian Publishing Company records 1895–1950, MS 6026, Box XX1A Lawson material, State Library Victoria.

2 Henry Lawson, letter to Bland Holt, 1902, in Colin Roderick (ed.), *Henry Lawson Letters 1890–1922*, p. 133.

3 Lynne McNairn, 'Manly – Seven Miles from Sydney and a Thousand Miles from Care', *Powerhouse Museum Photo of the Day*, 22 May 2014. http://www.powerhousemuseum.com/imageservices/2014/05/manly-seven-miles-from-sydney-and-a-thousand-miles-from-care/

4 Henry Lawson, letter to Bland Holt, 1902, in Colin Roderick (ed.), *Henry Lawson Letters 1890–1922*, p. 137.

5 Summons to Henry Lawson, 1902, in Lothian Publishing Company records 1895–1950, MS 6026, Box XX1A Lawson material, State Library Victoria.

6 Henry Lawson, 'Lawson's Fall', n.d., in *La Trobe Journal*, no. 70, Spring 2002, p. 52.

7 Bertha Lawson, letter to Henry Lawson, 14 December 1902, in Lothian Publishing Company records 1895–1950, MS 6026, Box XX1A Lawson material, State Library Victoria.

8 Henry Lawson, letter to *The Bulletin*, c. 1903, in Leonard Cronin (ed.), *A Fantasy of Man: Henry Lawson Complete Works 1901–1922*, p. 168.

9 Aubrey C Curtis (ed.), 'Reminiscences of Henry Lawson by Isabel Byers'.

10 ibid.

11 'Personal Gossip', *The Critic*, 28 February 1903, p. 6. http://trove.nla.gov.au/newspaper/article/212154580 Also quoted in Tasker and Sussex, '"That Wild Run to London"'.

Chapter 10

1 Bertha Lawson, letter to Henry Lawson, c. 1903, in Lothian Publishing Company records 1895–1950, MS 6026, Box XX1A Lawson material, State Library Victoria.

2 Brian Matthews, *Louisa*, McPhee Gribble, Melbourne, 1987, p. 71.

3 ibid., p. 97.

4 ibid., p. 87.

5 ibid., p. 77.

6 Colin Roderick, *Henry Lawson: A Life*, pp. 12–14.

7 Mary Gilmore, 'Personal History: Henry Lawson and I'.

8 Brian Matthews, *Louisa*, p. 127.

9 Henry Lawson, 'Table Legs, Wooden Heads and a Woman's Heart', *The Bulletin*, 30 March 1922, pp. 47–48. Also see Leonard Cronin (ed.), *A Fantasy of Man: Henry Lawson Complete Works 1901–1922*, p. 744.

10 Bertha Lawson, *My Henry Lawson*, pp. 153–154.

11 Denton Prout, *Henry Lawson: The Grey Dreamer*, p. 205.

Chapter 11

1 Henry Lawson, letter to Bertha Lawson, n.d., in Lothian Publishing Company records 1895–1950, MS 6026, Box XX1A Lawson material, State Library Victoria.

2 Bertha Lawson, letter to Henry Lawson, c. March or April 1903, in Lothian Publishing Company records 1895–1950, MS 6026, Box XX1A Lawson material, State Library Victoria.

3 Aubrey C Curtis (ed.), 'Reminiscences of Henry Lawson by Isabel Byers'.

4 Henry Lawson, letter to Bertha Lawson, n.d., Lawson family papers 1896–1968, MLMSS 7692 1 (1), State Library of NSW.

5 Henry Lawson, letter to George Robertson, 26 April 1903, in Colin Roderick (ed.), *Henry Lawson Letters 1890–1922*, p. 140.

6 Bertram Stevens, 'Henry Lawson'.

7 Aubrey C Curtis (ed.), 'Reminiscences of Henry Lawson by Isabel Byers'.

Chapter 12

1 Henry Lawson, 'The Separation', in *When I Was King and Other Verses*, pp. 75–76. Also see Leonard Cronin (ed.), *A Fantasy of Man: Henry Lawson Complete Works 1901–1922*, p. 158.

2 Colin Roderick, *Henry Lawson: A Life*, 1991, p. 252.

3 Aubrey C Curtis (ed.), 'Reminiscences of Henry Lawson by Isabel Byers'.

4 'The Divorce Court: Glimpse at Our Social Condition, Revelations in Numbers, &c.', *Evening News*, 16 September 1879, p. 6. https://trove.nla.gov.au/newspaper/article/107160077

5   NRS 13495 Divorce case papers #003 Mary Kirkham Wilson, 1873, State Records Authority of NSW.
6   Maintenance Order of the Court, in Lothian Publishing Company records 1895–1950, MS 6026, Box XX1A Lawson material, State Library Victoria.
7   *Matrimonial Causes Act 1873*, s. 22.
8   ibid.
9   *Matrimonial Causes Act 1899*, ss. 31–32.

Chapter 13
1   James Elphinstone, letter to Henry Lawson, 4 June 1903, in Lothian Publishing Company records 1895–1950, MS 6026, Box XX1A Lawson material, State Library Victoria.
2   This is an approximate count of divorce cases recorded from 1873 to June 1903 in NRS 13495, State Records Authority of NSW.
3   *Matrimonial Causes Act 1899*, s. 59.
4   Louisa Lawson, 'About Ourselves', *The Dawn*, vol. 1, no. 1, 1888, in Olive Lawson (ed.), *The First Voice of Australian Feminism*, p. 23.
5   Louisa Lawson, 'The Divorce Extension Bill or, The Drunkard's Wife', *The Dawn*, vol. 2, no. 11, 1890, in Olive Lawson (ed.), *The First Voice of Australian Feminism*, pp. 52–54.
6   ibid.
7   NRS 13495 Divorce case papers #4676 Bertha Lawson, 1903, State Records Authority of NSW.
8   'Personal Gossip', *The Critic*, 30 May 1903, p. 8. http://trove.nla.gov.au/newspaper/article/212155720

Chapter 14
1   NRS 13495 Divorce case papers #4676 Bertha Lawson, 1903, State Records Authority of NSW.
2   'Divorce Court', *The Sydney Morning Herald*, 5 June 1903, p. 8. http://trove.nla.gov.au/newspaper/article/14525554
3   ibid.
4   Bertha Lawson, *My Henry Lawson*, p. 81.

Chapter 15
1   Bertha Lawson, letter to Henry Lawson, 15 June 1903, in Lothian Publishing Company records 1895–1950, MS 6026, Box XX1A Lawson material, State Library Victoria.
2   Bertha Lawson, letter to Henry Lawson, 23 April 1903, in Lothian Publishing

Company records 1895–1950, MS 6026, Box XX1A Lawson material, State Library Victoria.

3   Benevolent Society of New South Wales records 1813–1995, MLMSS 6091, State Library of NSW.

4   Bertha Lawson, letter to Henry Lawson, 25 July 1903, in Lothian Publishing Company records 1895–1950, MS 6026, Box XX1A Lawson material, State Library Victoria.

5   ibid.

6   ibid.

7   *Royal Commission on the Decline of the Birth-Rate and on the Mortality of Infants in New South Wales*, Government Printer, Sydney, 1904.

8   Bertha Lawson, letter to Henry Lawson, 25 July 1903.

9   Sydney Benevolent Asylum Records, 1813–1995, MLMSS 6091, State Library of NSW.

10 Bertha Lawson, 'Memories', p. 117.

Chapter 16

1   Bertha Lawson, letter to Henry Lawson, 6 October 1906, in Lothian Publishing Company records 1895–1950, MS 6026, Box XX1A Lawson material, State Library Victoria.

2   Bertha Lawson, *My Henry Lawson*, p. 80.

3   ibid., p. 81.

4   Bertha Lawson, letter to Rose Scott, c. 1907, in Mrs Bertha Lawson correspondence 1895–1949, MLMSS 1639, vol. 6, State Library of NSW.

5   Olive Lawson (ed.), *Henry Lawson's North Sydney: A Selection of Henry Lawson's North Sydney Writings*, North Shore Historical Society, Sydney, 1999, p. 16.

6   Aubrey C Curtis (ed.), 'Reminiscences of Henry Lawson by Isabel Byers'.

7   Quoted in Denton Prout, *Henry Lawson: The Grey Dreamer*, p. 209. The excerpt is attributed to 'a note [Lawson] wrote'.

Chapter 17

1   Henry Lawson, 'To Jim', *The Bulletin*, 9 March 1905, p. 3. Also appears in *When I Was King and Other Verses*, pp. 188–190, and Leonard Cronin (ed.), *A Fantasy of Man: Henry Lawson Complete Works 1901–1922*, p. 197.

2   Henry Lawson, 'Barta', *The Bulletin*, 10 December 1903, p. 3. Also appears in *When I Was King and Other Verses*, pp. 186–187, and Leonard Cronin (ed.), *A Fantasy of Man: Henry Lawson Complete Works 1901–1922*, p. 161.

3   Bertha Lawson [Jago], unpublished notes.

4   ibid.

5   ibid.

6   Bertha Lawson, *My Henry Lawson*, p. 81.

Chapter 18

1   Henry Lawson, 'One Hundred and Three', *The Bulletin*, 26 November 1908, p. 39. Also appears in *The Rising of the Court and Other Sketches in Prose and Verse*, Angus & Robertson, Sydney, 1910, pp. 111–121, and Leonard Cronin (ed.), *A Fantasy of Man: Henry Lawson Complete Works 1901–1922*, pp. 371–374.

2   Deborah Beck, *Hope in Hell: A History of Darlinghurst Gaol and The National Art School*, Allen & Unwin, Sydney, 2005, p. 94.

3   ibid., p. 96.

4   Bertha Lawson, letter to Henry Lawson, 25 July 1903.

5   Australian Bureau of Statistics, 'Jobless Families', *Labour Force, Australia: Labour Force Status and Other Characteristics of Families, Jun 2011*, Cat. no. 6224.0.55.001, ABS, Canberra, 2011. http://www.abs.gov.au/ausstats/abs@.nsf/Products/6224.0.55.001-Jun%202011-Chapter-Jobless%20Families

Chapter 19

1   Henry Lawson, letter to David Scott Mitchell, 6 April 1905, in Colin Roderick (ed.), *Henry Lawson Letters: 1890–1922*, p. 148.

2   *Matrimonial Causes Act 1899*, ss. 42–43.

3   Henry Lawson, 'Going In', c. 1907, in Leonard Cronin (ed.), *A Fantasy of Man: Henry Lawson Complete Works 1901–1922*, p. 861.

4   Henry Lawson, 'Triangles of Life', in Leonard Cronin (ed.), *A Fantasy of Man: Henry Lawson Complete Works 1901–1922*, p. 285.

5   Henry Lawson, letter to George Robertson, 27 August 1908, in Colin Roderick (ed.), *Henry Lawson Letters: 1890–1922*, pp. 166–168.

6   Henry Lawson, 'The Song of a Prison', *The Bulletin*, 23 December 1909, p. 43. Also appears in Leonard Cronin (ed.), *A Fantasy of Man: Henry Lawson Complete Works 1901–1922*, p. 432.

7   Henry Lawson, letter to Bland Holt, 29 September 1909, in Colin Roderick (ed.), *Henry Lawson Letters: 1890–1922*, p. 176.

8   Henry Lawson, letter to Francis Sheriff Isaacs, February 1906, in Colin Roderick (ed.), *Henry Lawson Letters: 1890–1922*, pp. 149–150.

Chapter 20

1   Henry Lawson, letter to Isabel Byers, 26 September 1909, in Colin Roderick (ed.), *Henry Lawson Letters: 1890–1922*, p. 175.

2   'Paddington Tragedy – Trial of David Hanna – Charged with Murder',

The Australian Star, 20 May 1903, p. 5. http://trove.nla.gov.au/newspaper/article/228530374

3   Quoted in Deborah Beck, *Hope in Hell*, p. 125.
4   Norman Lindsay, 'Henry Lawson Reproves Bert Stevens', *Bohemians of the Bulletin*, p. 60.
5   Bertha Lawson [Jago], unpublished notes.
6   Bertha Lawson, letter to Henry Lawson, 15 June 1903.
7   Colin Roderick, *Henry Lawson: A Life*, 1991, p. 278.
8   ibid., pp. 293–294.
9   ibid., p. 265.
10 Olive Lawson (ed.), *The First Voice of Australian Feminism*, p. 54.
11 Bertha Lawson, letter to Henry Lawson, c. 1903, in Lothian Publishing Company records 1895–1950, MS 6026, Box XX1A Lawson material, State Library Victoria.
12 Henry Lawson, letter to Isabel Byers, 8 December 1909, in Colin Roderick (ed.), *Henry Lawson Letters: 1890–1922*, p. 181.
13 Aubrey C Curtis (ed.), 'Reminiscences of Henry Lawson by Isabel Byers'.
14 ibid.
15 ibid.
16 ibid. Also in Leonard Cronin (ed.), *A Fantasy of Man: Henry Lawson Complete Works 1901–1922*, p. 908.

Chapter 21

1   Bertha Lawson, letter to Henry Lawson, 2 January 1910, Lawson family papers 1892–1925, MLMSS 3694/Box 1/Folder 2, State Library of NSW.
2   Henry Lawson, letter to Bland Holt, 31 October 1909, in Colin Roderick (ed.), *Henry Lawson Letters: 1890–1922*, p. 177.
3   Henry Lawson, letter to Isabel Byers, 19 December 1909, in Colin Roderick (ed.), *Henry Lawson Letters: 1890–1922*, pp. 181–182.
4   Henry Lawson, letter to Isabel Byers, 5 January 1910, in Colin Roderick (ed.), *Henry Lawson Letters: 1890–1922*, p. 183.
5   Bertram Stevens, 'Henry Lawson'.
6   Aubrey C Curtis (ed.), 'Reminiscences of Henry Lawson by Isabel Byers'.

Chapter 22

1   Bertha Lawson, letter to Henry Lawson, 29 January 1910, Lawson family papers 1892–1925, MLMSS 3694/Box 1/Folder 2, State Library of NSW.
2   Jack Lindsay, *Life Rarely Tells*, Penguin, Melbourne, 1982, p. 54.
3   'An Artist Divorced – Norman Lindsay as Respondent', *The Age*, 21 June 1919, p. 14. http://trove.nla.gov.au/newspaper/article/155203134

4   Norman Lindsay, *Bohemians at the Bulletin*, pp. 58–59.
5   ibid., p. 59.
6   ibid., p. 41.
7   ibid., p. 59.
8   Bertha Lawson, letter to Henry Lawson, 29 January 1910.

Chapter 23

1   Henry Lawson, letter to Bertha Lawson, n.d. [February 1910], in Colin Roderick (ed.), *Henry Lawson Letters: 1890–1922*, p. 190.
2   Aubrey C Curtis (ed.), 'Reminiscences of Henry Lawson by Isabel Byers'.
3   Henry Lawson, letter to Jim Lawson, 22 March 1910, in Colin Roderick (ed.), *Henry Lawson Letters: 1890–1922*, pp. 192–193.
4   Bertha Lawson, letter to Henry Lawson, 17 February 1910, Lawson family papers 1892–1925, MLMSS 3694/Box 1/Folder 2, State Library of NSW.
5   Jim Lawson, letter to Henry Lawson, 22 December 1912, Lawson family papers 1892–1925, MLMSS 3694/Box 1/Folder 2, State Library of NSW.
6   Bertha Lawson [Jago], letter to Henry Lawson, 1912 (no exact date), Lawson family papers 1892–1925, MLMSS 3694/Box 1/Folder 2, State Library of NSW.
7   ibid.
8   Bertha Lawson [Jago], unpublished notes.

Chapter 24

1   Edward Tregear, letter to Bertha Lawson, 30 May 1911, Lawson family papers 1896–1968, MLMSS 7692 1 (1), State Library of NSW.
2   Henry Lawson, letter to W Ashe Woods, 15 July 1903, in Colin Roderick (ed.), *Henry Lawson Letters: 1890–1922*, pp. 140–141.
3   KR Howe, 'Story: Tregear, Edward Robert', *Dictionary of New Zealand Biography*, vol. 2, 1993, reproduced on *Te Ara – the Encyclopedia of New Zealand*, updated 30 October 2012. http://www.teara.govt.nz/en/biographies/2t48/tregear-edward-robert
4   Edward Tregear, letter to Bertha Lawson, 15 November [September?] 1911, Lawson family papers 1896–1968, MLMSS 7692 1 (1), State Library of NSW.
5   Edward Tregear, letter to Bertha Lawson, c. 1912, Lawson family papers 1896–1968, MLMSS 7692 1 (1), State Library of NSW.
6   Quoted in Bim Adewunmi, 'Do You Buy into Catherine Hakim's "Erotic Capital"?', *The Guardian*, 25 August 2011. https://www.theguardian.com/lifeandstyle/the-womens-blog-with-jane-martinson/2011/aug/25/catherine-hakim-erotic-capital
7   Alice McNamara, letter to Bertha Lawson [Jago], 5 February 1940, Bertha Lawson (Bertha Jago) papers, c. 1892–1980, MLMSS 3888/Box H1035, State Library of NSW.

8 Bertha Lawson [Jago], unpublished notes.
9 Ruth Park, *Fishing in the Styx*, p. 190.
10 ibid., p. 191.
11 ibid., p. 195.
12 ibid.
13 Bertha Lawson, *My Henry Lawson*, p. 4.
14 Bertha Lawson [Jago], unpublished notes.

Chapter 25
1 Henry Lawson, letter to George Robertson, January 1917, in Colin Roderick (ed.), *Henry Lawson Letters: 1890–1922*, pp. 261–263.
2 Henry Lawson, letter to George Robertson, 23 March 1917, in Colin Roderick (ed.), *Henry Lawson Letters: 1890–1922*, p. 317.
3 Ruth Park, *Fishing in the Styx*, pp. 193–194.
4 ibid., pp. 123–124.
5 Henry Lawson, letter to the Woman's Page, c. 1922, in Colin Roderick (ed.), *Henry Lawson Letters: 1890–1922*, p. 415.
6 Bertha Lawson [Jago], unpublished notes.
7 ibid.

Chapter 26
1 Mary Gilmore, note accompanying poem 'Ghost Haunted the Street He Goes', 23 February 1952, Lawson Collection (Lawson 164), Rare Books & Special Collections, Fisher Library, University of Sydney. Reproduced at https://library.sydney.edu.au/collections/rare-books/online-exhibitions/lawson/memories.html
2 ibid.
3 EJ Brady, 'Mallacoota Days', in Bertha Lawson [Jago] and J Le Gay Brereton (eds), *Henry Lawson by His Mates*, pp. 132–133.
4 Aubrey C Curtis (ed.), 'Reminiscences of Henry Lawson by Isabel Byers'.

Chapter 27
1 Bertha Lawson, letter to Mary Gilmore, n.d. 1922, Dame Mary Gilmore papers 1911–1954, A3292, State Library of NSW.
2 Zora Cross, 'Recollections of Henry Lawson', Lawson Collection (Lawson 204), Rare Books & Special Collections, Fisher Library, University of Sydney.
3 Mary Gilmore, letter to the editor, *Daily Mail*, 8 September 1922.
4 Rose Scott, 'Henry Lawson – To the Editor of the *Herald*', *The Sydney Morning Herald*, 14 September 1922, p. 6. http://trove.nla.gov.au/newspaper/article/16024824
5 Mary Gilmore, 'Personal History: Henry Lawson and I'.

6   ibid.
7   'Henry Lawson – State Funeral – Impressive Service', *The Sydney Morning Herald*, 5 September 1922, p. 10. http://trove.nla.gov.au/newspaper/article/16022883
8   Quoted in Denton Prout, *Henry Lawson: The Grey Dreamer*, p. 297.
9   Zora Cross, 'Recollections of Henry Lawson'.
10 Bertha Lawson [Jago], unpublished notes.

Chapter 28

1   Henry Lawson, 'The Romance of the Swag', c. 1907, in *The Romance of the Swag*, Angus & Robertson, Sydney, 1914. Also appears in Leonard Cronin (ed.), *A Fantasy of Man: Henry Lawson Complete Works 1901–1922*, pp. 65–68.